M000040570

'It is time to say what you mean.'
– Keith Gessen, *n+1* Issue 1 (Negation)

'The best goddamn literary magazine in America.'
– Mary Karr

'*n+1* is rigorous, curious and provocative. Intelligent thought is not dead in New York. It has simply moved to Brooklyn.' – Malcolm Gladwell

'[*n+1*] is decidedly youthful, not only in its characteristic generational concerns – the habit of nonchalantly blending pop culture, literary esoterica and academic theory, for instance, or the unnerving ability to appear at once mocking and sincere – but also in the sense of bravado and grievance that ripples through their pages.' – *New York Times*

Praise for *Say What You Mean: the n+1 anthology*:

'*Say What You Mean* . . . testifies to New York's fast-moving intellectual climate. The anthology is bold, aggressive and, at times, full of itself. But for a journal that aims to "lead the generational struggle against laziness and cynicism", it is fitting that it wears its heart on its sleeve.' – *Financial Times*

Christian Lorentzen is an editor at the *London Review of Books*.

The *n+1* Anthology – vol II

–

WHAT DO YOU DESIRE?

–

edited by Christian Lorentzen

Notting Hill Editions

Published in 2013 by Notting Hill Editions Ltd
Newcombe House, 45 Notting Hill Gate
London W11 3LQ

Designed by FLOK Design, Berlin, Germany
Typeset by CB editions, London

Printed and bound
by Memminger MedienCentrum, Memmingen, Germany

Copyright © 2013 by n+1 Foundation, Inc.
Poems reproduced in 'My Life and Times in American Journalism'
© Frederick Seidel, reproduced courtesy of the author

All rights reserved

The right of Christian Lorentzen to be identified as the editor of this work has been asserted in accordance with Section 77 of the Copyright, Designs and Patents Act 1998

This book is sold subject to the condition that it shall not, by way of trade or otherwise, be lent, resold, hired out or otherwise circulated without the publisher's prior consent in any form of binding or cover other than that in which it is published and without a similar condition including this condition being imposed on the subsequent purchaser

A CIP record for this book is available from the British Library

ISBN 978-1-907903-79-3

www.nottinghilleditions.com

Contents

Carla Blumenkranz

– Introduction –

I came to *n+1* the week after I graduated from college. I started as an intern at the second Brooklyn office, otherwise known as the Prospect Heights apartment of two of the founding editors, Chad Harbach and Keith Gessen. The apartment was also known, in emails, as 'headquarters'. This was June 2005, about the time that Christian Lorentzen's account of the magazine's beginning in the previous *n+1* anthology ends. The editors were working on the third issue, we were trying to figure out how to store subscriber information and put submissions in file folders, and the third roommate at the apartment, Brian, was sometimes doing push-ups in the next room.

It wasn't exactly what I had expected, but then again I didn't know what to expect. I had come across the first issue at St. Mark's Bookshop in the East Village, admired its spare, combative style, and sent an email to an address that I found on the magazine's at the time rudimentary website. This was a moment when small magazines seemed to make themselves very small and mostly only published fiction. I mostly wanted to read fiction but was thrilled by the possibility of a magazine that spoke plainly about the misery of contemporary politics, that knew how and why to condemn the recent turn toward literary preciousness, and whose writers believed their own lives were part of all this and worthy of deep and dispassionate observation.

During the next few months, Allison Lorentzen, the magazine's first managing editor (and Christian's sister), came by after her day job and talked to us about submissions. Sometimes Christian, an old friend of the editors who proofread and wrote film reviews, showed up and thought of terrible insults for the stories we were reading. On Bastille Day there was the first benefit party, at the Pink Pony in the East Village, and the interns were allowed to come for dessert. That summer was a time when I drank a lot of orange juice, which Keith and Chad constantly, somewhat guiltily offered us as we worked at their apartment for free. Probably the worst thing they did was go for a run and lock us out of the office. Probably the worst thing I did was accidentally create a Google Group, basically a reply-all, that included some large proportion of our subscribers. (I feel less bad in retrospect, as I look this up in email and realize how few subscribers we had that summer.)

The founding editors' project was beginning to include more people. Most notably, new writers were approaching the magazine's early preoccupations from entirely different perspectives. The fourth issue included four pieces about politics, nine essays on American writing, and multiple works by four fiction writers, as well as founding editor Mark Greif's *sui generis* 'Afternoon of the Sex Children' and Philip Connors's 'My Life and Times in American Journalism'. In total, the issue ran more than seventy pages longer than it was supposed to. One way of looking at this is that new pieces kept coming in and the issue kept not getting done; another is that the magazine wanted to become more expansive.

Connors's essay, which concludes this volume, is the exemplar. An account of a brief career in journalism, from the *Fargo Forum* to the *Wall Street Journal*, it describes the ideas and sensibilities out of which *n+1* emerged: that is, the dominant East Coast political and cultural climate in the years just before and after September 11, 2001. But because Connors had recently arrived from the Midwest, and also because of his training as a newspaper writer, he describes the excesses and losses of those years with a powerful sense of estrangement. Connors introduced a particular story to the magazine, one that has since been told several times over, about a young writer being educated at a large corporation. Five years later, Alice Gregory described writing catalog copy for contemporary works at Sotheby's. Gregory's piece opens with Sotheby's record-shattering Damien Hirst sale on September 16, 2008, the same day Lehman Brothers went bankrupt.

Subsequent issues saw more writers, who tended toward the idiosyncratic, treat the evolving realities of the magazine's founding preoccupations. A. S. Hamrah, formerly an editor of *Hermenaut*, a defunct little magazine out of Boston, came on as our film editor and spent two months in 2007 watching thirty-six films about the war on terror. Hamrah's default mode is a deadpan moral scrutiny, and he seems to have hated almost every minute of it, but a few films made the difference. '*Iraq in Fragments* is so good,' he wrote, 'I'm surprised people even recognize it as a movie.' Molly Young, who came to *n+1* as an intern, and with a gift for tactile description, described taking Adderall so candidly and viscerally she made anyone who hadn't want to try it. Young's piece marked the arrival of a slightly later generation, who had taken different drugs, started out writing online, and in subsequent years surprised us by seeing *n+1* – when they arrived as readers or writers or volunteers, or started their own magazines – as part of the literary establishment.

Nikil Saval was one of the interns on the first day in Prospect Heights, but on the second day we heard he had quit for a full-time job as an editorial assistant in the book business. The next time I saw him he was bartending the third-issue party; he was going to find a way to help out at *n+1* after all (and not only by bartending). A day job with a corporate publisher turned out to be a poor substitute for the work he had been willing to do for free. Still Nikil kept going to the office, and then another office, and then another, and as he wrote in his first piece for the magazine, when you spend most of your time in an office, you also spend an extraordinary amount of time thinking about them. 'Birth of the Office' describes how architects' and designers' best attempts at liberating white-collar workers from the physical strictures of their offices are undone by the actual corporate restraints that define most American workplaces. The essay (the basis for a book Nikil recently finished, which will appear next year) suggests what a person might find to save himself in a collective enterprise like a small magazine: 'the ability to produce and control our own work, in lines with the ends of a community we support and love'.

In early 2006, we moved the *n+1* office out of Brooklyn and into half a room in a warehouse building on Chrystie and Stanton. This was in an area that at the time had not been claimed by the Lower East Side, Chinatown, or Soho, that had a nightclub and a liquor warehouse, but that now also has the New Museum and generally is considered part of the Lower East Side. We were subletting our half of the room from the person on the other side of a makeshift wall, Mark Weinberg. Mark designs album covers. He had drawn the logo for Naughty by Nature and was known to stay out till dawn with Joe Strummer. He mostly worked at night but might enter or emerge from his office at any time during the day, in moods that ranged from jovial to apparently quite depressed. If you stayed late enough you could smoke a joint with him or see the guy who actually lived on our hall and sometimes would walk through it wearing only a towel. We heard that the Talking Heads had lived on the top floor twenty years earlier and later found out that a respected artisanal pickle impresario had his office in the building at the same time and in fact remains there to this day. In 2008 we moved our office, with Mark Weinberg's, to Dumbo, where then there were other magazines and nonprofits and now there mostly seem to be start-ups, and last year Mark moved to San Diego.

Nikil and I came on as apprentices at a time when the magazine was still in the early stages of its development. For years it remained unclear whether *n+1* would move past that point, whether we would find the time and money to publish more regularly and the next set of generative questions that would give us new things to say. More income, from magazine sales and some donors, helped (and would still help for that matter), but what really made the magazine feel like a sustainable project was an infusion of energetic new editorial actors. This was in 2010, when Christopher Glazek and Elizabeth Gumport came on as assistant editors and Dayna Tortorici started as an (indefatigable) intern. At the same time, Mark Greif was creating the research branch of the organization, which so far has encouraged young volunteers and editors to pursue independent work on the radical feminism of the early seventies, contemporary literature in Central and South America, and the influence of internet pornography on sexual attitudes and behavior. The next fall marked the beginning of the Occupy movement, which again reinvigorated our, and many others', understanding of what we could communally accomplish.

The younger editors' work is represented here by Christopher Glazek's 'Hasids vs. Hipsters', about the warring subcultures of gentrifying South Williamsburg. The essay first appeared in *What Was the Hipster?* (2010), part of the *n+1* book series, which has occasionally put out titles since the magzine's founding and will publish several in the coming year. Chris's own provocative lucidity has appeared with even more extremity in the magazine, in recent essays on the American prison system and class mobility. In 'Raise the Crime Rate', Chris made the point that the violent crime that has largely disappeared from American cities has simply been displaced into remote, overcrowded prisons. 'The nation's prisons now contain more inhabitants than any American city save New York, Los Angeles, and Chicago,' he wrote. 'And yet there is no "prison correspondent" at any of the nation's major newspapers.'

Chris's essay on American class mobility ran in the Intellectual Situation, the opening polemical section that has defined *n+1* since its founding. Always unsigned and often collectively written, the section has addressed dating, online bookselling, urban gentrification, global warming, and other subjects we can mostly agree are currently shaping our shared circumstances. In one recent issue, Elizabeth, Dayna, and I took the entire section to describe the intersection of gender, digital, and financial anxieties at traditional general interest magazines, most notably the *Atlantic* and *Harper's*. 'What do women have to do with the internet?' we wrote. 'We submit that, in the eyes of media executives, women *are* the internet. Women, we mean the internet, are commanding a larger share of the traditional print market. The internet, we mean women, is less responsive to conventional advertising than to commenting, sharing, and other forms of social interaction,' and so on. We were speaking directly about the magazines we read and indirectly about the one that has become our own. The first Intellectual Situation set the bar for subsequent issues as it denounced the 'regressive avant-garde' at *McSweeney's*, the narrowness of the *New Republic*'s book critics, and the merging of postmodern theory and cynical politics at the *Weekly Standard*. As ours surveyed the current magazine landscape it introduced the possibility that a new feminism and a rational approach to the internet could define *n+1* as well.

Three essays collected here – Kristin Dombek's 'How to Quit', an ambivalent memoir of addiction; Lawrence Jackson's 'Slickheads', an account of growing up black in Baltimore written in local dialect; and Emily Witt's 'What Do You Desire?', about the politics of the porn industry and the new ethics of sexual experimentation – were all published in the past year. Something that gives us pride is that we doubt these essays could have appeared anywhere else. Dombek and Jackson work at universities and for the most part have produced academic writing, while Witt makes her living as a freelance journalist for mass-circulation publications. The work these writers most want to do has no real place in their ordinary careers, and that's why *n+1* goes on.

Emily Witt

– What Do You Desire? –

On a Monday last April, I stood in line at JFK Airport to board a plane to San Francisco. Before me stood a silver-headed West Coast businessman. His skin had the exfoliated, burnished sheen of the extremely healthy; his glasses were of an advanced polymer; he had dark jeans. He wore the recycled ethylene-vinyl acetate shoes that are said never to smell. His fleece coat was of an extraordinary thickness and quality, with a lissome external layer that would not pill. He seemed like the sort of man who would pronounce himself a minimalist and say that everything he bought was selected for its extraordinary craftsmanship and beautiful design. But the silver fox's computer bag was a cheap thing with netting and buckles that said GOOGLE on it. The person in front of him in line wore a Google doodle T-shirt with Bert and Ernie where the Os would be. In front of him was a Google backpack.

Until I left San Francisco it never went away. It was embroidered on breast pockets, illustrated with themes of America's cities, emblazoned on stainless-steel water bottles, on fleece jackets, on baseball caps, but not on the private coach buses that transported workers to their campus in Mountain View, where they ate raw goji-berry discs from their snack room and walked about swathed, priestlike, in Google mantles, with Google wimples and Google mitres, seeking orientation on Google Maps, Googling strangers and Google chatting with friends, as I did with mine, dozens of times a day, which made the recurrence of the logo feel like a supremacist taunt.

My first day in the city I sat in a sunlit café in the Mission District, drank a cappuccino, and read a paper copy of the *San Francisco Chronicle* that lay anachronistically on the counter. I overheard someone talking about his lunch at the Googleplex. 'Quinoa cranberry pilaf,' I wrote down. And then, 'coregasm.' Because that was the subsequent topic of discussion: women who have spontaneous orgasms during yoga. The barista was saying how wonderful it was that the issue was receiving attention, coregasms being something a lot of women experienced and were frightened to talk about. Those days were over.

The people of San Francisco were once famous for their refusal of deodorant and unnecessary shearing. Sometimes, walking down the street, past gay construction workers and vibrator stores, I was reminded that this was the place where Harvey Milk was elected (and assassinated), where the bathhouses had flourished (and closed). But most of the time I noticed only that the people of San Francisco appeared to have been suffused with unguents and botanical salves, polished with salts, and scented with the aromatherapeutics sold in the shops that lined Valencia Street. The air smelled of beeswax, lavender, and verbena, and the sidewalks in the Mission glittered on sunny days. The food was exquisite. There was a place in Hayes Valley that made liquid-nitrogen ice cream to order. I watched my ice cream magically pressured into existence with a burst of vapor and a pneumatic hiss. This miracle, as the world around me continued apace, just moms with Google travel coffee mugs talking about lactation consultants. Online, people had diverted the fear of sin away from coregasms and toward their battles against sugar and flour. 'Raw, organic honey, local ghee, and millet chia bread taming my gluten lust,' was a typical dispatch. 'Thank goodness for ancient grains.'

At night I was alone, and I would walk down the street listening to sermons in Spanish from the storefront churches and the electronic hum of the BART train below. The city was a dream world of glowing screens and analog fetishism, of Google, orgasms, stone fruits, and sparkles. A Greek chorus of the homeless and mentally ill connected these fragments into deeper conspiracies, until I began to see conspiracies myself. I would walk down the sidewalks of the Mission and note their glittery resemblance to my powdered blush in its makeup compact. 'This sidewalk looks like Super Orgasm,' I would think, Super Orgasm being the name of the particular shade of blush I own. My makeup reveled in contemporary sexual politics: FOR HIM

& HER read the sticker on the back of my paraben-free foundation. I contemplated a possible economic index comparing the cost of a pint of honey-lavender ice cream to the federal minimum hourly wage. I ran to Golden Gate Park, where giant birds of prey gazed hungrily upon glossy dachshunds. The cyclists passed in shoals, dressed in Google bicycle jerseys.

I had never had a coregasm and my sexual expectations conformed to widely held, government-sanctioned ideals. I was single, and now in my thirties, but I still envisioned my sexual experience eventually reaching a terminus, like a monorail gliding to a stop at Epcot Center. I would disembark, find myself face-to-face with another human being, and there we would remain in our permanent station in life: the future.

In San Francisco, people thought differently. They sought to unlink the family from a sexual foundation of two people. They believed in intentional communities that could successfully disrupt the monogamous heterosexual norm. They gave their choices names and they conceived of their actions as social movements. I had come to San Francisco to observe this sexual vanguard, but I did not think their lessons applied to me. 'But what is your personal journey?' they would ask, and I would joke about this later with my friends.

Public Disgrace is an online pornography series that advertises itself as 'women bound, stripped, and punished in public.' It is the creation of a 30-year-old San Francisco-based porn director and dominatrix named Princess Donna Dolore. Princess Donna conceived of the project in 2008, during her fourth year of working for the pornography company Kink.com. In addition to directing, Donna performs in the shoots, though she is not usually the lead.

When Princess Donna is scouting locations for *Public Disgrace* she looks for small windows (they need to be blacked out) and spaces (they need to look crowded). For outdoor shoots she usually works in Europe, where public obscenity laws are more forgiving. Before each shoot, Princess Donna coordinates with the female lead to establish what she likes or doesn't like and produces a checklist of what the performer will take from her civilian audience. Some models are happy only with groping, some have rules against slapping, and some are willing to go so far as to be fingered or spit on by the audience.

For female performers, the draw of *Public Disgrace* lies in Donna's directorial prowess. Princess Donna is an experienced orchestrator of complicated fantasies of group sex, public sex, and violent sex. Such situations tend to be, as Princess Donna puts it, 'kind of tricky to live out in real life.' She is also a deft manipulator of the human body. Female performers trust her to extend the boundaries of their physical capacities.

The job description for *Public Disgrace*, posted at Kink.com, reads: 'Sex between male dominant and female submissive; domination by female and male dom; secure bondage, gags, hoods, fondling, flogging, and forced orgasms with vibrators.' For four to five hours of work, performers earn between $1,100 and $1,300, plus bonuses for extra sex acts with cameo performers who can show a clean bill of health.

A week after I arrived in San Francisco, I attended a *Public Disgrace* shoot. The shoots are open to the public, a public that's encouraged to actively participate. Novelty is important to the world of porn, so audience members are recruited through the internet but restricted to attending one shoot a year.

The venue of the shoot I attended, a bar called Showdown, was on a side street haunted by drug addicts and the mentally ill just south of the Tenderloin, next to a Vietnamese sandwich shop and a flophouse called the Winsor Hotel (REASONABLE RATES DAILY-WEEKLY). When I arrived, several people were standing under the red arrow outlined in yellow lightbulbs above the entrance, waiting to get in, including a group of young men and a heterosexual couple in their thirties. We signed releases, showed our photo IDs, and a production assistant took a mug shot of each of us holding our driver's license next to our face. Then she gave us each two drink tickets that could be redeemed at the bar. 'Depending on how wasted everyone seems to be I will give you more,' she promised.

That evening's performer, a diminutive blonde who goes by the stage name Penny Pax, flew up to San Francisco from her home in Los Angeles especially for the *Public Disgrace* shoot. She had told Donna that one of the first pornos she ever watched was*Public Disgrace*, and since she got into the business herself she had been anxious to make one. Her personal request for the evening was that Princess Donna attempt to anally fist her.

The bar was a narrow room with a sense of history attached to it, of an older San Francisco that was a working-class mix of Irish and Italian immigrants. Old-fashioned smoked-glass lamps hung over the wooden bar. A color-copied picture of Laura Palmer from David Lynch's television show *Twin Peaks* hung on the wall, next to a stopped clock with a fake bird's nest in the cavity where a pendulum should have been. Behind the front area with the bar was a dark square room with black wallpaper patterned with alternating illustrations of two parrots on perches and a vase of flowers. The crew from Kink had rigged lighting overhead.

Princess Donna arrived with a small entourage, wearing a vacuum-tight black minidress that flattered her exceptionally perfect breasts. Donna is an extraordinary physical presence in any group of people, and her stature plays integrally into her authority. She is five foot seven with long, almost alarmingly thin limbs that make her seem taller. She has large, brown, Bambi-ish eyes that, the night of the shoot, were complexly shadowed and wreathed in fake eyelashes, which Kink purchases in quantities of several hundred at a time. Her long brown hair was tied up in a high ponytail. She has a tattoo of a biologically correct heart on her left shoulder and a cursive inscription that says DADDY on her inner right forearm. She strode into the room carrying a black vinyl purse from which a riding crop protruded. With her minidress she wore tan cowboy boots, which made the length of her legs appear heron-like. A neck bruise the size of a silver dollar that I had noticed during my first meeting with her a week before had faded.

Donna stood before the bar with the palindromically stage-named male performer, Ramon Nomar, surveying the room. He pointed up to several hooks on the ceiling and to a metal Juliet balcony over the bar. Donna nodded without a word. They retreated to the back. I asked a production assistant where the female performer was. Penny Pax, she said, was having 'quiet time.'

Soon, the music was silenced (Kink had its own music, cleared of rights, to play). The bartender removed his gingham shirt and his tie and suddenly was wearing nothing but his waistcoat. Donna came out to make some announcements to the assembled crowd, which was well on its way to getting soused.

'You might think we are doing things to the model that are mean or humiliating, but don't,' said Donna.

'She's signed an agreement.' According to the agreement, the crowd had permission to poke the model, fondle her, and finger her, but only if they washed their hands and had neatly trimmed fingernails. A fingernail trimmer was available if necessary. 'I'm going to be watching you like a hawk to make sure you're not doing degrading things to her pussy,' Donna said. She continued: 'You're allowed to spit on her chest but not her face. You can give her a hard spanking but you are not allowed to give her a hard smack.' She pulled her production assistant over to her physically. 'If Kat is the model' – here Kat bent over obligingly – 'this would be a reasonable distance from which to spank her.' Donna mimed responsible spanking practice.

The model, Donna went on to explain, could not leave the set bruised because she had another shoot coming up this week. Donna said that therefore at some point she might have to forbid certain practices to ensure Penny's body remained unmarked.

Donna concluded her speech with a more theoretical exposition. The whole point of *Public Disgrace*, she explained, is that it's supposed to seem spontaneous, and that 'you guys are not supposed to know that we're coming here.' Taking video was forbidden, photographs with phones were fine, but the most important thing: 'Don't ignore us. I'm going to walk her in with a sign that says I'M A WORTHLESS CUNT. So react to that.' She repeated that nail clippers and files were available for anyone who wanted them and reminded the audience to wash their hands in the bathroom before touching the model. Then she returned to the back room.

A few minutes later Donna emerged with Penny Pax and Ramon in tow. Penny was small, just over five feet tall, with full natural breasts, milky white skin, and a chin-length bob of cornsilk blond. Her eyes were the rich azure of a blue raspberry Blow Pop. She was very pretty, and decidedly not plastic or spray-tanned. She looked like a model in a JCPenney catalog. She wore a denim miniskirt, white high heels, and a white tank top. Donna looked her over, then deftly pulled the straps of Penny's tank top off her arms and folded them down. She spun Penny around, unhooked her white padded bra, and tossed it to one side. From a black duffel bag under a table Donna picked up and put back various coils of rope, judging the weight and length of each one. Meanwhile Ramon stared – the only word for it is *lovingly* – at Penny's breasts, which hung pendulously down, stretch marks visible. Grabbing them, Donna executed a complicated-looking tie, uplifting the breasts to bra elevation by winding the rope around each one. She pulled the straps of Penny's tank top back over her shoulders, then tied Penny's arms behind her back.

'Look at that,' said Donna, surveying her work and turning Penny around. 'You look gorgeous.' Meanwhile Ramon stepped in and looked over Penny with the tender carnivorousness of a dime-store bodice-ripper. He ran his hand over Penny's body from behind, turned her around and examined her, kissed and inhaled her hair, then put his hand up her skirt and began feeling her while staring intently at her body. This was his way of preparing for the shoot. Ramon was from Spain and had a sharp accent. He rarely smiled. He wore a tight black T-shirt that showed off his impressive pectorals, black pants, and black combat boots. He was just over six feet tall, tan, and sculpted like an Iberian Bruce Willis. This was an attractive couple. Donna hung a sign, which indeed read I'M A WORTHLESS CUNT, around Penny's neck, then grabbed Penny roughly by the hair and took her out the door.

Now the cameras were recording. Now we could redeem our drink tickets. The bar was full, mostly with men. These men I would divide into two groups: the openly slavering, confident about the righteousness of their lust, and the self-conscious, worried about breaking the taboos of touching and insulting a woman. They were joined by a smattering of females, some of whom were there with their boyfriends, others who had come together in pairs. Donna had exchanged her cowboy boots for patent leather high heels and now strode through the door purposefully, she and Ramon on either side of Penny, who looked up at her tall handlers with baleful blue eyes.

'Tell everybody why you're here,' ordered Donna, as the people drinking at the bar feigned surprise. 'I'm a worthless cunt!' said Penny. Using some kind of professional wrestling trick, Ramon lifted her up by her neck and sat her on the bar. Working together, Donna and Ramon stuffed a cocktail napkin in her mouth and taped it into a gag, taking turns slapping her on her face and her breasts. They ripped off her spotless white tank top. The rope had cut off circulation to Penny's breasts and they looked painfully swollen.

'Who wants to touch it?' asked Donna. 'Who wants to play with this worthless little cunt?' The bar patrons obligingly hit, fingered, and spanked her. From her handbag, from which the riding crop still menacingly protruded, Donna now withdrew a device that crepitated electric sparks and started shocking Penny with it. Ramon removed what remained of Penny's clothes, then his belt, and began gently swiping it at Penny, who was soon pinioned on the floor.

'I thought it was your dream,' goaded Donna. 'I thought it was your dream to shoot for this site. You didn't come ready?' She looked around the room. 'What's her name?' she demanded. 'Everyone knows what her name is.'

'Worthless cunt!' yelled the crowd.

'What pretty girl wants to grab her titties?' A woman in attendance obliged. Ramon took off his pants, balancing on each foot as he pulled them over his combat boots. He was not wearing any underwear; his penis looked like the trunk of a palm tree. The bar patrons burst into applause.

He picked Penny up and had sex with her against

the bar as the extras continued to smack at her breasts. Penny, still gagged, was wide-eyed. Her mascara had begun to run in rivers down her face. She had the option of halting everything with verbal and nonverbal cues but she did not exercise it. Suddenly Donna stopped the show. 'Everyone, I have an announcement,' Donna said, as she removed the ropes still tied around Penny's breasts. 'No more smacking this boob,' she said, pointing to the right one, which had red marks on it. They resumed shooting.

Ramon, who had biceps like cannons, hoisted Penny around the room and the crowd followed, vying with one another for a good sightline. He was able to walk around holding Penny in one arm, wielding the zapper in the other. 'Zap me!' requested a male audience member. Ramon rolled his eyes and did so without breaking rhythm. 'Ouch,' said the guy, looking sore. Ramon removed Penny's gag and guided her into a blowjob, during which Penny theatrically gagged. Donna stood by, slapping and shocking, and then tag-teamed in. Using her hands, she made Penny ejaculate, to the delight of the crowd. After fifteen or twenty minutes, Donna called for a break.

Paused in the middle of his exertions Ramon looked up at the ceiling with a look of super-intense concentration. Penny was on the floor. He picked her up and sat her on the bar. He and Donna tenderly tucked her hair back from her face and wiped off her sweat and the grime from the floor with Cottonelles.

Donna, like a trainer during a boxing match, removed Penny's false eyelashes, gave her water, and kissed her on the cheek. During this reprieve from shooting, the crowd, which had been as verbally abusive as directed, seemed sheepish.

'You are beautiful and I'd take you to meet my mother!' yelled one man who had been particularly enthusiastic about yelling 'worthless cunt.' Ramon asked for a drink. 'What do you want?' said the bartender. 'A soda,' said Ramon. 'Porno guy wants a soda!' echoed the loud man.

When shooting resumed, a female audience member, heavily tattooed and wearing a miniskirt and a ragged T-shirt that had two skeletal hands printed across her breasts, had a go at Penny's body. Things continued in this way for more than an hour. Chairs were knocked over. Drinks were spilled. The bartender had by now removed his vest and was shirtless. The crowd was drunk and excited, although not entirely unembarrassed. 'Make that bitch choke,' shouted the shouty man. Then: 'Sorry!'

Donna began to wind things down. 'OK guys,' she said, to prepare the audience, 'the pot shot's not the end though.' The crowd cheered. With the cameras off, Ramon and Penny had vanilla missionary sex on a table to get to the point where he could ejaculate. He nodded when he was ready, then put Penny on the floor, and masturbated until he came on her face. Again the room burst into applause.

The performers took a break. Ramon's job was now done. With the room's attention focused on Penny he yanked off his sweaty T-shirt, flung it into a corner, and wandered off into a dark part of the bar, naked but for his combat boots. Like a long-distance runner who has just crossed the finish line, he walked it off, moving his arms in circles, wiping the sweat from his face with his arm, and taking deep breaths. Nobody noticed him. Eventually he recovered his composure, toweled off, and put his black jeans back on. Penny, meanwhile, rested primly on a chair and sipped water. Her expression was, in a word, elated.

I joined Donna at the bar. What was going to happen next?

'I want to get my hand all the way in her ass,' she said. 'She's never done that before and she wants to try it.'

Princess Donna sat Penny Pax down on a bar table. She had a Hitachi Magic Wand and a bottle of lubricant. 'I need all the room that's in her holes for my hand,' she announced, and the audience deferentially took a step back. After Donna accomplished her task, the crowd chanted, 'Squirt, squirt, squirt, squirt,' and then Penny did. I watched all this from a corner, standing next to Ramon, who had a towel around his bronzed shoulders and was drinking a bottle of pilsner.

Shooting was coming to a close. Donna and Ramon moved Penny back to the bar and strung her up by her wrists to the metal balcony. I saw Donna in a corner, carefully wiping down a beer bottle with a sanitizing wipe. And that was the final shot of the evening: Penny tied up and suspended from the railings of the balcony by her wrists, while a member of the audience penetrated her with a beer bottle. Ramon, now shirtless and in jeans, casually sparked the zapper across his pectoral muscles a couple of times, then reached out and zapped Penny on the tongue she offered to him with a scream. Then it was done. With a debonair flourish, Ramon effortlessly picked up the tiny starlet and carried her out of the room in his arms.

Kink interviews its female performers before and after every shoot. It's a de-escalation strategy that reminds the viewer – if he watches it (Kink does not release the demographics of its audience, but studies have found that 98 percent of paid porn is watched by men) – of the controlled conditions of what he just watched, and confirms that the activity was consensual and that the model has recovered. Penny wandered out for her postgame interview wearing pink glasses, a gray bathrobe, and a pair of Uggs. But for her smeary mascara, she looked like a college student on her way to a dormitory bathroom. Donna arranged Penny's bathrobe to reveal her breasts. Other than that, like most postgame interviews with athletes, this one was a little bland.

DONNA
So, Penny, how did you enjoy the shoot this evening?

PENNY
I had a great time, it was amazing. There was so much going on.

HECKLING AUDIENCE MEMBER #1
I actually want to take you out for lunch later!

HECKLING AUDIENCE MEMBER #2
You have really pretty eyes!

DONNA
All right everybody, hold on. Tell me what your favorite parts were.

PENNY
Probably, uh, just the getting handled by everyone and not really knowing how many hands were on me, or who was touching me . . . And then the – I don't know, did you get your fist in my butt?

DONNA
I did.

PENNY
Well, that was awesome. Yay! I can't wait to see it!

DONNA
Yeah, that was rad. Round of applause for the anal fisting! (*Audience applauds.*)

DONNA
And you also said that you had never squirted like that before?

PENNY
Yeah, that was ridiculous. How did you do that?

DONNA
Magic fingers. Years of practice.

PENNY
Yeah, it was amazing.

DONNA
What were the most challenging parts?

PENNY
Uh, probably putting your fist in my butt? That was pretty challenging. It felt really full.

DONNA
On a scale of one to ten, how would you rate your happiness leaving the shoot?

PENNY
Eleven! (*Applause. Whistles.*)

DONNA
So is it safe to say that you would come back and shoot for the site again?

PENNY
Yes.

DONNA
Do you want a shower?
(*Penny Pax nods.*)

DONNA
Let's get you a shower!

MALE AUDIENCE MEMBER
A golden shower!

FEMALE AUDIENCE MEMBER
Can I come?

After this conclusion, Penny and I retreated to a stairwell behind the bar. Penny, I learned, is 23 years old. I asked if she had been working in the industry since she was 18. No, she said, she wishes. She had only been in the industry for six months. Before working in porn she was a lifeguard in Fort Lauderdale. Being a lifeguard in Fort Lauderdale had been pretty boring. I asked her about the shoot. I wanted to know how it had felt.

'It's a little uncomfortable in the beginning, for the anal,' she said. (She was presumably referring to a moment early in the shoot when Ramon jumped up on the bar, stuffed a lemon in Penny's mouth, and had anal sex with her. 'Nice boots, man!' someone in the audience yelled. Penny made a nonverbal cue to slow down and Donna jumped over and slathered her with lubricant.) 'But my body warms up pretty quickly and then there's no discomfort.' Slightly incredulous, I asked if there were moments then of genuine pleasure. She looked at me like I was crazy. '*Yeah*. Like the whole thing! The whole thing.' She apologized for not being more articulate and explained she was in a state of delirium. 'We call it "dick drunk."'

I rode back to the Mission in a van with Donna and Penny and Ramon. Penny and Ramon were both sleeping over at the landmarked Moorish castle that houses Kink. They usually work in mainstream porn in San Fernando Valley, but enjoy coming to San Francisco. In the shoot he was doing tomorrow for New Sensations in Los Angeles, Ramon lamented, they wouldn't even let him pull the girl's hair. I surmised that making more extreme pornography if you're a performer is like wanting to write like Beckett if you're a writer.

I left Penny and Ramon wandering the lobby in their gray bathrobes and stepped out into the cold San Francisco night. I walked west to Valencia Street, where I found a scene of unexpected destruction. Broken glass filled the sidewalks. The windows of every storefront – TACA Airlines, an adjacent property management company, the boutique after that, and on down the street – had been shattered. The windshields of the cars lining the street had been systematically bludgeoned. A new apartment complex under construction had FUCK THIS SHIT spray-painted on a column. I stared at the hanging fragments of glass and the garbage bins tipped over on the sidewalk. Then I crossed to the undamaged side of the street and bought myself an ice cream sandwich. I asked the cashier what had happened. He described a dozen protesters dressed in black. The following day was May 1. I knew strikes were planned in Oakland, but on this side of the Bay nobody had seemed particularly interested in Occupy Wall Street.

I took some photos of the destruction and posted them to the websites of the great technology corporations with written exclamations of bafflement. Then I deleted the posts. I tried to think about the sex I had just watched. In the early years of broadband internet, *Frontline* had made a documentary called 'American Porn.' ('It's a multibillion-dollar industry – and growing. In a wired world, can anything stop it?') After interviewing various porn industry stalwarts, the male anchor had attended a shoot not unlike the one I just watched and had walked out in disgust. While I certainly worried about what I had seen, I could not find it in myself to feel that level of indignation. I ate my ice cream sandwich and went to sleep.

Over the course of the next several weeks I watched Princess Donna direct and star in more films. I watched her perform in a roller-derby-themed episode of a series called *Fucking Machines* where she wielded a drill retrofitted with a giant dildo. I watched her train for her new role as director of a Kink property called *Ultimate Surrender*, a girl-on-girl wrestling tournament. For three eight-minute rounds, two women wrestled each other. The goal was for one woman to pin the other and molest her for as long as possible. For the fourth round, the winner has sex with the loser wearing a strap-on dildo. It's one of Kink's most popular properties and is sometimes shot before a live studio audience. Princess

Donna also directs a series called *Bound Gangbangs*, and one day was inspired to do a shoot where all the men were dressed as panda bears. I watched this too, and was surprised to find it beautiful.

I, personally, was not having sex while all this was going on. Not that the sex I would've had, if I'd been having sex, would've been anything like the sex that was going on at the Kink castle. The Kink actors were more like athletes, or stuntmen and -women performing punishing feats, and part of what fascinated me was the ease with which they went in and out of it, the comfort with which they inhabited their bodies, their total self-assurance and sense of unity against those who condemned their practice. I possessed none of those qualities.

I had made no conscious decision to be single, but love is rare and it is frequently unreciprocated. Because of this, people around me continued to view love as a sort of messianic event, and my friends expressed a religious belief that it would arrive for me one day, as if love was something the universe owed to each of us, which no human could escape. I had known love, but having known love I knew how powerless I was to instigate it or ensure its duration. Whether love was going to arrive or not, I could not suspend my life in the expectation of its arrival. So, back in New York, I was single, but only very rarely would more than a few weeks pass without some kind of sexual encounter.

What even to call these relationships? Most of my friends had slept with one another and I had slept with many friends, too. Sometimes years separated sexual encounters. Things thought buried in the past would cycle around again, this time with less anxiety and greater clarity, in a fluid manner that occasionally imploded in horrible displays of pain or temporary insanity, but which for the most part functioned smoothly. We were souls flitting through limbo, piling up against one another like dried leaves, circling around, awaiting the messiah.

After a decade or so of living this way, with occasional suspensions for relationships that would first revive my belief in romantic love and its attendant structures of domesticity, and then once again fail and extinguish them, I started finding it difficult to revere the couple as the fundamental unit of society. I became a little ornery about it, to be honest: that couples paid lower taxes together, that they could afford better apartments, that there were so few structures of support to ease the raising of a child as a single person, that the divorced experience a sense of failure, that failed marriages are accompanied by so much logistical stress on top of the emotional difficulties. All this because we privilege a certain idea of love. The thought of the natural progression of couples, growing more and more insular, buying nicer and nicer furniture, shutting down the world, accruing things, relaxing into habit, scared me. As I grew older, I found it difficult to distinguish romantic love from other kinds of connections: the platonic love for the friends I did not want to have sex with, the euphoric chemical urges toward people I had sex with but did not love. Why was love between couples more exceptional? Because it attached itself to material objects, and to children? Because it ordered civilization? I probably would not have a baby without love, and buying a home seemed impossible for all kinds of reasons, but I could have sex. I had a body.

A few weeks before I decided I should go to California and watch people make porn, this revised outlook toward my prospects – that I did not need to see my life as an unanswered question, in permanent suspension for the answer of a relationship – resulted in deliberate immersion in New York's sexual fray. A relationship had ended, I kept running into old friends, I was internet dating; it was all happening. Then all of it imploded. First, I inadvertently caused someone emotional devastation. Second, I was told I might have been exposed to chlamydia. Third, I therefore might have given chlamydia to someone else. Fourth, and this really was the worst part, I received an email from an acquaintance that accused me of destroying her friend's relationship.

The next day, sitting in the packed waiting room of a public health clinic in Brooklyn for the un- and underinsured, I watched a clinician lecture her captive, half-asleep audience on how to put on a condom. We waited for our numbers to be called. In this cold, adult daylight, I examined what I had done. I thought about the suggestion, in the email from my acquaintance, that

I 'stop pantomiming thrills' and 'starkly consider the real, human consequences of my real-life actions.' A single person's need for human contact should not be underestimated. Surrounded on all sides by my imperfect fellow Americans, I thought many were also probably here for having broken some rules about prudent behavior. At the very least, I figured, most people in the room knew how to use condoms.

The clinician responded with equanimity to the occasional jeers from the crowd. She respectfully said 'no' when a young woman asked if a female condom could be used 'in the butt.' After her lecture, while we continued to wait, public health videos played on loop on monitors mounted on the wall. They dated from the 1990s, and dramatized people with lives as disorderly as mine, made worse by the outdated blue jeans they wore. The brows of these imperfect people furrowed as they accepted diagnoses, admitted to affairs, and made confessional phone calls on giant cordless phones. Men picked each other up in stage-set bars with one or two extras in fake conversation over glass tumblers as generic music played in the background to signify a party-like atmosphere, like a porn that never gets to the sex. They later reflected on events in *Real World*-style confessional interviews. From our chairs, all facing forward in the same direction, awaiting our swabbing and bloodletting, we witnessed the narrative consequences. (One of the men has a girlfriend! And gonorrhea! Now he has to tell his girlfriend that he's bisexual *and* that he has gonorrhea!) The videos did not propose long-term committed relationships as a necessary condition of adulthood, just honesty. They did not recriminate. The New York City government had a technocratic view of sexuality.

The federal government had different expectations. Following the phone call I had looked up chlamydia on Google, which led me to the website for the Centers for Disease Control and Prevention. The government suggested that the best way to avoid chlamydia was 'to abstain from vaginal, anal, and oral sex or to be in a long-term mutually monogamous relationship with a partner who has been tested and is known to be uninfected.' Porn might be a fantasy, but at least it is not a fantasy that defies all interpretation. The suggestion of abstinence came with a more realistic reminder to use condoms. I usually used condoms, but this time I had not used a condom, so now I used antibiotics. When the lab results came back weeks after my visit to the Brooklyn clinic it turned out I did not have chlamydia. None of us had chlamydia.

Still, I didn't have sex again for nearly seven months.

The women at Kink came to porn for various reasons. Bobbi Starr, a 29-year-old who won *Adult Video News*'s Female Performer of the Year award in 2012, was raised in a Pentecostal Christian family in San

Jose, California, and was homeschooled until middle school. She trained as a swimmer, competed in the Junior Olympics, and earned a scholarship to study music at San Jose State University. Although she had always considered herself sexually adventurous, she was 22 years old and working as a classical musician when she watched porn for the first time. Sitting down with a male friend, who was surprised at her lack of awareness, she watched several videos, including one called *Bong Water Butt Babes*. Very little needs to be said about this video except that the bedroom set is covered in sheets of plastic. Starr was mesmerized, applied for a job at Kink, enjoyed the bondage work, and within a year got an agent and moved to Los Angeles.

I asked her about pain. She recalled an 'authentic BDSM experience' she had with a Kink dominatrix named Maitresse Madeline. 'I had my head in the pit and she was flogging me and caning me and single-tailing me and doing all these really, really intense corporal activities with me and then she started tickling me and I just completely broke,' she said. 'At some point I came out and just cried on her chest and then she started crying.' She described the experience as cathartic. 'Through her dominating me and me subbing to her we had this really unique experience. I think that she and I are better partners, we have a better working relationship because of it, I think we have a better friendship because of it, I think it's easier for us to communicate.'

One day, I watched Princess Donna have her makeup done for a shoot with the porn phenom James Deen. (The first male porn star of the internet age to amass a vocally enthusiastic following among women, James Deen's popularity seems explicable not by his slight physique but by the way he gazes at his partners and whispers urgently in their ears – he manages to convey genuine, ardent desire. In real life he reminded me of the boy in the eighth grade who went around snapping girls' bra straps.) Another model wandered in, a lanky woman wearing hot pants and a bra that enclosed each breast in its own beribboned dirndl. A tattooed tendril of morning glories climbed the length of her very long leg. Donna introduced her to me as Rain DeGrey, and told me that she, Donna, had directed Rain's first shoot five years ago.

We went into a sort of lounge in the next room that had wall-to-wall carpeting and sofas. On one sofa a young woman with wet hair, wearing a gray bathrobe, barely out of adolescence if at all, sat painting her toenails a vivid sapphire. Her stage name was Katherine Cane. Rain DeGrey sat on a chair in front of me, applying sedimentary layers of Jergen's bronzer as we talked.

Rain DeGrey described herself as a '24–7 lifestyle kinkster' and 'pansexual.' She told me that for years she had denied the fact that bondage and flogging turned her on. She knew that even in the Bay Area it was not something you could just tell people, that she would be judged for her preference.

'Finally you're like, 'Hey, it's OK if normies think I'm a freak,'' she told me. 'And the day that I came out as kinky I felt fifty pounds lighter.' One day, she was tied up in her local dungeon, The Citadel, getting flogged by a friend, when someone suggested she try to do some of this stuff professionally.

Her first shoot was for the Kink site Wired Pussy, which at the time was under Donna's direction. For the first scene they shot together, Donna stood over Rain DeGrey with a cattle prod. Donna told her if she moved the shoot would end.

'I don't know if you've ever tried to sit still on your hands and knees and not move while someone cattle prods you,' said Rain.

Five years later, Rain DeGrey, who does not have a college degree, has bought herself a four-bedroom house with her earnings from Kink. She is very grateful to Donna for her counsel and support.

'I was actually on set for her *Bound Gangbangs* that she did, where she took on eight dicks.' Rain stood up. She proceeded to demonstrate a play-by-play of everything that had happened, which ended with Donna on the floor, 'this little, limp, sweaty, fucked rag doll. James Deen's just kicking her as hard as he can and she loves it.'

Rain DeGrey returned to her chair and resumed her ceaseless application of self-tanning lotion. The chemical baby-powder scent of it wafted over us. I said nothing.

'I don't know if you've ever had cum in your eyes?' she asked.

'No,' I said.

'That's like a super-duper hard limit for me,' said Katherine Cane, shaking her head in dismay.

'It blinds you,' said Rain.

'It stings horribly,' said Katherine.

'Do you realize the dedication that takes?' asked Rain. 'That's how committed she is.'

Committed to what? To getting guys sitting in their studio apartments to jerk off to you for $30 a month? Not an insignificant accomplishment, but enacting a fantasy of violence for personal reasons was one thing; doing so for money was another. I held my tongue, and Rain continued.

'We're told our entire lives how fragile and delicate our bodies are,' she said. She adopted a tone of mock concern. "Don't go out late at night, someone might mug you.' 'You've got to be careful, bad things will happen to you.' And there's a certain liberation in challenging your body, and getting beaten or distressed in some way and realizing you're actually tougher than you realized.'

She looked over at Katherine, who had finished her pedicure and had her toes out in front of her. 'Know what I mean?'

'Exactly,' Katherine responded.

'It is a very empowering experience to realize you're not as fragile as you've been told your whole life,' said Rain.

'But it's just as empowering to let yourself break down, in my opinion, because you go to a place that is so vulnerable and scary that a lot of people don't want to acknowledge it because it's your weakest point possible,' said Katherine.

'The vulnerability,' agreed Rain.

'Like you're safe to be your completely base, your most broken-down, crying, you can't even talk.'

I didn't say anything, but here's what I thought: there was no great truth about the human condition that I would discover through celibacy.

Princess Donna makes a lot of porn: on average she does a couple of shoots a week, and she's been directing for eight years. Unsurprisingly, she sometimes gets bored and wants to try something different. When Princess Donna proposes a project, her boss, Kink CEO Peter Acworth, must approve it. Sometimes there are conflicts. Early in her career Donna proposed doing a series called *Dirty Girls*, which she described to me as 'like girl–girl sex, but like rough sex, but not with, like, a dom/sub relationship but just like going at it, with like fisting and spitting and dunking people's heads in toilets, lots of anal, stuff like that.' Acworth decided not to give the green light, but Kink thought the request was interesting enough that they posted an online debate between Donna and Acworth.

PETER
So the fisting is really the most important thing to you.

DONNA
Clearly a lot of people like fisting and girls dominating each other and spitting on each other. It's still pretty extreme.

PETER
I don't know how much for the male customers . . . you know for the male viewer I don't know how much fisting actually adds to it.

DONNA
I've had so many male viewers ask me for fisting. Like on Insex [Donna's previous employer] when I worked there they were always like, yeah, 'fisting fisting fisting fisting.' I think there's a lot of guys who think fisting is hot. I think *you* don't think it's hot.

Donna then proposed a lesbian gangbang site, which also did not pass, and then started experimenting with the tactics that would go on to become *Public Disgrace*. She started while still filming *Wired Pussy*, doing a series of shoots in New York where she would wire up the performer and shock her under her clothes in public places. These were popular, so Donna did a *Wired Pussy* shoot where she invited members of the public. Eventually she got the go-ahead to make *Public Disgrace* a recurring series.

I had insisted to myself that I wanted a long-term, committed relationship, of the kind celebrated by the CDC and most happy endings (of the narrative sort). I had decided that any other kind of sexual relationship was a 'waste of time.' Having committed myself to a limited worldview I saw not as limited but rather as dignified and adult, I was able to distance myself from the very question I had gone west to investigate – one that was turning into a major question of my adult life: if love could not be relied upon to provide an idyllic terminus to one's sexual history, and naive performative attempts at a noncommittal sex life resulted only in health scares and hurt feelings, how best to still carry out a sexual existence?

In San Francisco, the right to be a lawfully wedded couple was not taken for granted, but this question was still pursued with a cheerful, pragmatic determination. It came accompanied by Google spreadsheets, jargon, discussion groups, community centers, dietary changes, and hallucinogens. San Francisco's sexual vanguard might overuse words like 'consciousness' and 'mindfulness,' but the success of their politicization of sex had repercussions that reached across the country. The mind-set could sometimes seem grim, or at least all that talking kind of dampened the feeling of spontaneity. But they meant it: 'Polyamory is a decolonizing force,' one person explained to me. 'If you want to transform society, it includes our intimate relations.'

I met with everyone I could. I met a group of

Google employees in their early twenties, beneficiaries of the country's most elite educational institutions, now applying their sharp minds to the investigation of multiple concurrent relationships. They all did yoga, were extremely attractive, and accompanied their sexual experimentation with controlled consumption of psilocybin mushrooms and MDMA. They spoke of primary and secondary relationships, and described a world in which jealousy and possessiveness were the sins to overcome. I attended the cult-like meetings of a group of people who have devoted themselves to the female orgasm. After a 'game' at one meeting, where I stood directly in front of a male stranger who looked in my eyes and repeatedly demanded answers to the question 'WHAT DO YOU DESIRE?' for several minutes, I went home, drank almost a full bottle of wine, and wept.

I took the train across the Bay to Oakland for a quiet dinner with several anarchists, to talk about anarchist ideas of sexuality. They all wore black and spoke of their decisions with a seriousness that my friends in New York might have had derided. The anarchists cooked kale and dressed their pasta with cashew pesto from a jar. Oakland's soft summer warmth came as a welcome relief from San Francisco's miserable microclimates. We dined with the windows open and the evening sun flooding into an apartment lined with books.

In another part of Oakland I met with a radical queer activist who had a platonic partner, a sexual partner, and a rotating cast of people with whom she 'played.' (The really tough part, she admitted, was the scheduling.) I asked if her platonic partner was not just her roommate, or a friend, but she explained that it involved a deeper commitment: going to holidays at each other's family homes, caring for each other when sick – everything expected of a husband or wife except for the sex. It wasn't any easier than marriage, either: they were in couples' therapy.

In the past twenty years, in San Francisco especially, the celebration of choice over systems has coincided with the advent of new technology and an influx of money and entrepreneurs. One result has been the healthy, humane workplaces presented by Google, Facebook, Twitter, and the other Bay Area companies and their acceptance of individual expression in the corporate workplace and of families in all their forms. These changes made for a better working experience, but they also made it easier to complacently watch the flourishing of unfamiliar digital monopolies, to partake in the consumer delights produced by unprecedented inequality with a mistaken sense of political agency, and to pay to watch a woman get gangbanged on the internet with a clean conscience, because the producers used the rhetoric of the fair and just. The ghosts of the formerly ostracized, including the untimely dead, haunted the city. The general consensus was that we honored the dead and the formerly oppressed by enacting the present utopia.

The wealth and the corporate culture that produced it defied the old models of good and bad. Google's motto, 'Don't be evil,' had been adopted across a range of industries. Evil, unfortunately, remained loosely defined: we would know it when we saw it. But all we saw on our computers were our photographs, our friends, our broken hearts, our writing, our search terms, our sexual fetishes.

The friendly blandness of Google's interface bestowed blessing on the words that passed through its sieve. On Google, all words were created equal, as all ways of choosing to live one's life were equal. Google blurred the distinction between normal and abnormal. The answers its algorithms harvested assured each person of the presence of the like-minded: no one need be alone with her aberrant desires, and no desires were aberrant.

Googling 'tiny blonde tied up and ass fucked in public' will lead you to a video I saw recorded in San Francisco one April evening. In life, the sex I saw there did not upset me, but when I arrive at the video via Google I want to turn it off. The whole motivation of our new sexual paradigm might be to ensure that nobody will be alienated, but porn is a medium where the expression of one person's happy sex life can easily shade into another person's estrangement.

I watched how my friends became anxious when the subject of porn came up. Some people enjoyed watching it as part of a daily routine. Some felt enslaved by their desire for it. Others saw their real-world sexual experiences reduced to a corny mimicry of porn, and wished they could somehow return to a time when porn was less ubiquitous, or was just soft-focus tan people having relatively unadventurous sex by a swimming pool. Since more men watch porn than women, the occasional imbalance of knowledge caused distress all around and was perceived at times as an imbalance of power. Porn made people jealous, it hurt feelings, it made them worry about whether their partners were attracted to them, or to the kind of people they watched in porn, who might have a different color hair, skin color, or bra size. Because porn loves the taboo, it was also sometimes racist and misogynist.

It's tempting to think that life before internet porn was less complicated. There are sexual acts in porn that it would not occur to many people to attempt. We have more expectations now about what kind of sex to have, and how many people should be involved, and what to say, and what our bodies should look like, than we might have at a time when less imagery of sex was available to us. But if the panoply of opportunity depicted in porn seems exaggerated, the possibilities are no less vast outside the internet. The only sexual expectation left to conform to is that love will guide us toward the life we want to live.

What if love fails us? Sexual freedom has now extended to people who never wanted to shake off the old institutions, except to the extent of showing solidarity with friends who did. I have not sought so much choice for myself, and when I found myself with no possibilities except total sexual freedom, I was unhappy. I understood that the San Franciscans' focus on intention – the pornographers were there by choice – marked the difference between my nihilism and their utopianism. When your life does not conform to an idea, and this failure makes you feel bad, throwing away the idea can make you feel better.

The panda gangbang took place deep in the basement of the Kink armory, where rivulets of the long-suffocated Mission Creek still trace a path between moisture-eaten columns, and the air hangs heavy with a stony dampness. On the day of the shoot, a glow of warm light punctured the center of a cavernously empty space. Bathed in this warm glow, a young woman named Ashli lay sleeping, impervious to the stygian immensity of her surroundings. Her sleek black hair was draped over her shoulder; a small silken bow of the palest pink pinned it away from her face into a girlish side part. The hem of her pink dotted-swiss dress had been carefully arranged to reveal a glimpse of her upper thigh through the gauze. On her feet she wore six-inch patent leather high heels embellished with lace. She slumbered on a bed of green leaves in a simulated bamboo forest beneath wraiths of mist produced by a Rosco Hazemaker puffing gently away beyond the circle of light, the sound of which seemed not to disturb her.

The panda bears approached her from behind. They waved their horrible paws and sniffed inquisitively. One stood over her nibbling at a frond of bamboo. Another gently stroked her hair.

'Now poke her or kick her,' ordered Donna from the darkness. The pandas fell upon her. The sound of ripping gauze and a snapped bra strap broke the quiet. They fondled and slapped at her now-exposed breasts. She awoke and screamed in fear. 'But I love pandas, I love pandas!' she cried out.

The panda shoot was a taxing one. Donna hovered around the bears, using metal clamps to keep the furry folds of their costumes from hiding the action. They took turns with Ashli without conferring much. Finally the pandas retired to their bamboo bowers and the shoot was over.

[2013]

A. S. Hamrah

– Jessica Biel's Hand –

THE CINEMATIC QUAGMIRE

For two months this summer the only movies I watched were movies about the war on terror. While other moviegoers were enjoying cinematic treats like *You Don't Mess with the Zohan* and *The Happening*, or the revival of Kobayashi's *The Human Condition*, or that Norwegian movie about Norwegian yuppie writers that everybody liked so much, I was immersed in the backlog of global-war-on-terror movies released since 2002. The only summer blockbuster I saw was *Iron Man*, a war-on-terror movie and therefore allowable.

I watched three dozen of these movies and maybe 15 percent of them were any good. The rest, like the war itself, represented an enormous waste of manpower and resources that would have been better spent on something good for people, like entertainment. When I say this I do not mean any disrespect to the three thousand men and women who died on September 11, 2001, or the over four thousand American soldiers who have died overseas, or the tens of thousands of Iraqis who have been killed, or the unknown number of detainees who have been tortured in prisons. But watching these movies was like being buried under rubble while working in an office, like being stuck in the desert far from home, invaded by an occupying army, left tied in a stress position for days.

You ask why I put myself through this. Like some kid fresh out of high school sauntering into a recruitment center just to check it out, I wasn't exactly coerced. I wasn't drafted. A suggestion was made, I volunteered, I didn't want to seem like a wuss. Here was the story of our time, they said, told cinematically. Wasn't it my duty to cover it? It might be, I answered. So they signed me up, they put my name on a contract.

Fortunately for me, I cannot be stop-lossed. American soldiers continue to die in Iraq with no power to make it end, but I can simply file this report, turn my back on the cinematic quagmire and walk away. I know it's unfair. It's criminal. But if there's one thing we've learned these past seven years, it's that fairness has nothing to do with it.

The first Iraq war movie was *Fort Apache*, a western John Ford made in 1948. It was also the first Vietnam movie. A thinly veiled retelling of Custer's defeat at Little Bighorn in 1876, *Fort Apache* holds up the ordinary cavalry soldier, represented by John Wayne's Captain York, against an oblivious commander, Henry Fonda's Colonel Thursday, who foolishly leads his men to doom at the hands of Apache warriors. In *Fort Apache*, the soldiers of the Seventh Cavalry do their duty, 'riding the outposts of a nation,' as it says in another Ford western, while a commander who refuses to listen to his officers charges blindly into death.

Wayne's York gives what amounts to a press conference after the defeat. He doesn't lie to the assembled reporters who consider the dead Thursday a hero – we can't picture John Wayne lying in a movie made in 1948 – but he doesn't tell the truth, either. What he does is let the reporters believe what they want to believe. The reporters don't really listen to what York says, anyway. Instead, they tell him what happened in the battle, even though they weren't there and he was. York's response, a soliloquy about dead soldiers and the permanence of the US Army, delivered by John Wayne as he looks out a window, ends the film.

The Apaches carry *Fort Apache*'s moral weight, rejecting peace to fight with honor. The movie preserves the dignity of the US Army, however, which is portrayed as separate and apart from Thursday's stupidity even as it's subject to it. Ford shows Thursday was wrong; he shows how regular soldiers get killed. What makes the film tragic is that it doesn't matter. In their victory the Apaches remain the enemy, in defeat Thursday remains a hero. After a while nobody remembers the dead soldiers' names.

John Ford fought in World War II and filmed the landing at Normandy, but *Fort Apache* was not about the war just ended. It was about a much longer war.

What we see in movies about the war in Iraq and Afghanistan, in movies about the so-called global war on terror, is that we are still playing the Fort Apache game – cowboys and Indians and reporters.

Maybe another film, made closer to the events at hand, a film with no moral weight at all, is really the first Iraq war movie. In 2001, less than four months before the destruction of the World Trade Center, *Pearl Harbor* came out, to much fanfare, on 3,200 screens.

Brought to us by the men who made *Armageddon*, *Pearl Harbor* existed to celebrate, in costly and spectacular fashion, the fliers who avenged the attack that got us into World War II. But it also existed to do away with the very idea of moral weight, to make war look like late-'90s action-adventure, something that happens while Ben Affleck and Josh Hartnett argue over a girl. In *Pearl Harbor* Michael Bay and Jerry Bruckheimer celebrated war from the sky, a kind of war like the first Gulf War, the kind Jean Baudrillard could claim didn't really take place because the soldiers fighting it were never in any danger.

Who wants to remember *Pearl Harbor* now? After seven years of this new war that isn't so new anymore, nobody does. Looking back on that obnoxious and innocent time when *Pearl Harbor* was the first blockbuster of 2001, and being able to see the last blockbuster of that summer looming on the horizon, *Pearl*

Harbor becomes an insult to everything – life, death, war, the movies. Why was that entertainment?

The truth is it wasn't entertainment. Is any summer blockbuster? Summer blockbusters are civics lessons, collective work we do for the economy, grim torture-filled slogs like *The Dark Knight* or the war in Iraq. The lesson of *Pearl Harbor* came in the form of dialogue delivered by Colonel Jimmy Doolittle, played by Alec Baldwin in the last role he had where we were supposed to take him seriously as an authority figure. 'Victory belongs to those who believe in it the most and believe in it the longest,' he says in *Pearl Harbor*. 'We're gonna believe. We're gonna make America believe, too.'

In the year or so before 9/11 that's what all our blockbusters were telling us, from *X-Men* to *Bring It On*. It was a message we were ready to hear. Boys and girls had to get together as a team, learn from the old dudes, and kick some ass. Why? We didn't know why. But it's good to be prepared.

Soon enough we found out. And pretty soon after that, just like in *Duck Soup*, we had a war we were promised would be both easy to win and endless.

Right away entertainment began to take over. Already there was no other way to see anything. Everything had to fit into the world of entertainment, even though TV, the source of entertainment, kept saying the world had changed forever.

On September 11, 2001, two French brothers, Gédéon and Jules Naudet, who were working on a documentary about a firehouse in downtown New York, filmed the destruction of the World Trade Center right from Ground Zero. They caught the planes going into each tower, the initial rescue efforts, with the sound of bodies thudding on the pavement outside. Jules Naudet, trapped with firemen inside the North Tower when the South Tower collapsed, continued filming.

It was like filming the exact moment of the Big Bang, but in reverse: the end of the world. The buildings were gone, there was nothing but white smoke and sirens. Spreadsheet confetti fell endlessly, like volcanic ash. 'The building collapsed to dust,' says one firefighter in *9/11*, the TV movie that emerged from the Naudets' footage. 'No desks, no chairs, no telephones, no computers . . . you find a foot.'

The footage is frightening and tragic, put together in a thoughtful way that gives every firefighter his due, and yet something's missing. You feel bad for even thinking so, but it's true: something's missing. The Naudets' footage, as essential as anything that's ever been filmed, became the basis for a TV special. Set within the context of TV it strives to be really good TV, and it is really good TV, and now who ever thinks about the Naudets or their footage anymore?

While Jules Naudet was filming in the North Tower, a thousand miles away, in Sarasota, Florida, George W. Bush was sitting in front of an elementary school classroom reading along with second graders as they followed a story called 'The Pet Goat.' After his chief of staff whispered to him that a second plane had struck the Twin Towers, the President just sat there for over seven minutes. He continued to read silently or stared into space.

This footage is as essential as the Naudets' footage of the end of the World Trade Center. It too deserves to be seen in its entirety. Instead, it was taken over by Michael Moore, who was afraid we would be bored by it. So instead of letting us see this thick chunk of dead time in which the President of the United States squirmed, he spoiled it in *Fahrenheit 9/11* by showing only sections of it, adding an on-screen countdown clock to time the President's inaction, and talking over it, telling us what we were already seeing: 'Mr. Bush just sat there.'

Whatever we would have thought about this footage on our own was not good enough for Michael Moore. He ruined it in the name of entertainment, encouraging us not to think while he showed pictures of a man he claimed wasn't thinking.

The first twenty-five minutes of Oliver Stone's *World Trade Center*, which take place on the morning of

September 11 before the first tower was hit, are an evocative and even beautiful remembrance of New York City – evocative and beautiful because we know what's going to happen. Haunted shots accumulate and create a strange tension the rest of the film can't sustain. Stone wisely introduces the towers from the deck of the inbound Staten Island Ferry; we see that romantic view that is gone forever. Soon the shadow of a plane passes over the side of a building with a billboard for the movie *Zoolander* on it.

World Trade Center has the unintentional effect of reminding us how much TV we watch. So much of the film consists of families of trapped policemen watching TV that you begin to see this as a fundamental part of Stone's view of humanity. History is a slag pile they stare at without understanding. (The firemen called Ground Zero 'the Pile.') Stone forces regular people to watch and rewatch the catastrophe over and over, as if he's saying, 'See? See?' He makes his characters submit docilely to TV news, then presents the rest of their lives as a series of Hallmark moments that weren't worth filming.

These are the tropes of war-on-terror movies: fake Middle Eastern music, constant TV news and radio commentary, scenes of combat shot in Morocco instead of Iraq, actors we don't recognize speaking Arabic with subtitles, videos of men in ski masks proclaiming in

Arabic while they hold a Westerner hostage, American soldiers accidentally killing an Iraqi woman or child, vets losing their shit in their hometowns, a constant resort to cell phones, a scorpion fight, titles identifying every location change, a cut to black to avoid showing something horrible, a precredits wrap-up crawl that tells us what happened later, blonde wives back home. It's amazing how everyone has a blonde wife back home. You'd think al Qaeda made these movies.

Shaky-cam always reminds me of TV cop shows or coffee commercials, things that are on in the background. There's a lot of shaky-cam in *United 93*, so like TV it has an ambient quality. It's almost calm. A storm is brewing but all people do is look at computer screens and talk on cell phones. Then they turn on CNN. Back on the plane, a hapless passenger is buttering a muffin while one of the hijackers puts together a bomb in the restroom.

The hijacker's bomb is a fake meant to frighten the passengers into submission, a prop in the movie but a prop in real life, too. It makes you think about how all the cell phones in the movie are props. The actors scream and cry into their fake phones, yet they are not famous actors, maybe not actors at all, and you put yourself into their situation so much you can't believe they actually made a movie about this. If Kevin Costner were on the plane, you might have cheered it on its way, wanting it to crash as he calmly dialed his wife. His presence would have contradicted this strange radio commentary from the Naudets' *9/11*: 'What you see here is right out of one of those movies you would see in Hollywood: people walking around with cell phones in tears.' The cell phones cried that day and it seemed like Hollywood.

United 93 is an exploitation film in the form of a safety-instruction manual. It manipulates us mercilessly but blandly. When Flight 93 crashes the screen cuts to black. The only decent thing to do at that point would have been to end the film right there and flip on the lights in the theater. But miles of credits roll like they always do.

Robert Redford's *Lions for Lambs* is as close to the purely didactic as Hollywood gets. Yet since it doesn't quite know what it wants to say, this salutary didacticism is really a lost cause. It's like a play that examines every viewpoint it can think of in the most boring way possible. I admired that about it, but if it were a person doing that instead of a movie, you'd leave the room. Maybe the same thing does happen with the movie. It's hard to imagine someone watching it. It's like an art installation called 'Robert Redford Political Movie.' Tom Cruise is exceptional as a US senator who wants to escalate the war. For some reason, he's very good at playing very serious self-convinced loonies. Redford, however, gives the scariest aging-star performance since *What Ever Happened to Baby Jane*? At one point, while calmly discussing something with a student in his office (he plays a college professor), he suddenly jerks his hand upward to reveal a huge scar on his forehead, then barks out lines about getting 'fifty-four stitches protesting in Chicago' after he came home from Vietnam. That was as harrowing as the plane crash in *United 93*. It was so unexpected and frightening I jumped out of my seat like it was wired. I know he's an actor playing a part and all, but in the 1960s Robert Redford was a handsome movie star who made a lot of money by not being in Vietnam. I don't know if he was at the 1968 Democratic National Convention, but somehow I doubt it. Wasn't he filming *Butch Cassidy and the Sundance Kid* then? He thinks we all have short memories. That's probably why we allowed another Vietnam to happen.

The American cinema has been producing bullshit for so long now it's no longer capable of dealing with a situation like this. That's the message of *Home of the Brave*. The vets in this movie who return home and have trouble adjusting to civilian life are a sad mirror for Hollywood's inability to cope with the war in Iraq. In *Home of the Brave*, one of the vets even gets a job selling tickets at a cineplex. 'I sell these stupid tickets to these stupid movies,' he says. 'But I don't go see any of them.'

In 1946, right after the war, William Wyler cast a

man named Harold Russell in *The Best Years of Our Lives*, a movie about the problems vets faced returning to their hometowns. Russell, an army vet, was a nonactor who lost both hands in an explosion during the war and was fitted with prosthetic hooks. When you watch the movie you can tell Russell is not a professional actor yet his performance as sailor Homer Parrish is unsentimental, affecting, and unforgettable.

In *Home of the Brave*, pretty Jessica Biel plays a vet who has lost one hand. The actual Jessica Biel, it goes without saying, has both her hands. Her stump, which we see, is a prop stump she covers with another prop, a fake hand. When a coworker at the school where she teaches gym tries to help her with something by saying, in all seriousness, 'Hey, let me give you a hand,' the audience laughs. If somebody had laughed at Harold Russell in 1946, he would've gotten his head bashed in. That is the difference between then and now – not just in terms of how we think about veterans or about the current war, but about the movies too, about whether acting is taken seriously and about the way actors move through the frame or are moved through the frame by directors. The story in 1946 was that Harold Russell's Homer was a good guy who faced his problems the only way he knew how, by trying to get through life like everybody else. In the film from 2006, there is no story; there is a message. The message is that if you lost a hand in Iraq, Jessica Biel might play you in a movie. Any veteran who laughed at her deserves a medal.

There is a difference between acknowledging that many veterans come home with post-traumatic stress disorder and wanting them to come home with it. Fortunately for Hollywood, many vets do come home with psychological problems, emotional adjustment issues that lend themselves to drama. *In the Valley of Elah*, which is based on a true story, is noteworthy for how sordid and amoral it is, how sordid and dull.

Paul Haggis, who wrote and directed it, seems to have consciously drained the film of all the effects that ruin contemporary filmmaking. *In the Valley of Elah* is quiet, low-key, precisely framed and carefully lit, shot in long takes. It has things besides Tommy Lee Jones in common with *No Country for Old Men*: its brutality and its southwestern setting. Jones is better in this than in the Coens' film. He gets to be typically authentic but also an uptight asshole. He's got a face like a dog, with black beady eyes, jowls and lines, and he looks shrunken, pale, and mottled. An excellent actor named Victor Wolf, who plays a Latino soldier from Jones's son's unit, gets to spit a question in Jones's face: 'Wouldn't it be funny if the devil looked just like you?'

When the film sticks to amorality it's pretty good. When it gets to lecturing Salvadoran janitors about raising American flags upside down to signal distress, it gets pretty bad. The film refuses to condemn the war outright. It does so instead by equation. The war must be wrong if it turns a soldier's best buddies into psychos who will kill him for no reason, then chop him up and set him on fire to get rid of the evidence. This is a case where 'based on a true story' really works for Hollywood. It gets you to shut up and keep your complaints to yourself.

Empires in decline need imaginary cads who are also superheroes. They send them out into the world preening and being casually brutal so we can all pretend the empire's doing fine. The English have James Bond, a 1960s import to the movies from postwar British fiction, and now America has Robert Downey Jr.'s Tony Stark, a.k.a. Iron Man, an import from our literature created in the Vietnam era and updated for the war in Afghanistan.

Because of Robert Downey's charm we care only about Tony. When he puts on the Iron Man suit we lose interest; he becomes a steroidal C-3PO and he's gone. But Tony Stark fascinates. He needs a fake heart to keep him alive, the fake heart powers a superhero carapace that makes him all-powerful – he's a metaphor for how Hollywood movies work at the box office. The metal suit is as much an excuse to give Robert Downey a good part as it is a touching industrial fantasy. Tony Stark and Iron Man are two separate things. When he's out of the suit, he's free, he can act, do interesting things other actors don't do when they play superheroes because they are always too much the costume. What's also touching is Tony Stark's very American desire to make everything right in the world, a desire he doesn't share with James Bond.

To the extent that *Iron Man* is a war movie about how Yankee ingenuity and super-technology will make things right in Afghanistan, it's interesting. When it becomes a clash between competing business executives in giant metal suits, it's boring. And when Tony Stark returns home and asks for a hamburger after being tortured and held captive in the caves of Tora Bora, and somebody gives him one from Burger King, and Robert Downey has to act like he likes it, you have to wonder what's the point of being a billionaire playboy at all.

Grace Is Gone is a curious film. It had the potential to be the best of the homefront Iraq war movies – certainly it's the best acted. It's under eighty minutes long, but that's not its problem. The problem is that it gives every indication of having been tampered with or left slightly incomplete. Scenes seem truncated, and actors in the cast list aren't really in the movie. It emerges as a film that was worth making, wasn't fully made, and is only half worth watching.

Another problem has to do with one of the film's locations, a small amusement park that to me was clearly a substitute for Disney World. It's too bad Disney World would never let a film like this be made there.

That would be something, a poignant indictment more to the point than a lot of documentaries. It's too bad in general that although going to Disney World is a big part of a lot of people's lives, it's an experience that can't be represented cinematically outside of home movies. God forbid we should see somebody unhappy on the spinning teacups.

John Cusack plays a schlumpy, tentative Home Depot manager in the Midwest who doesn't know how to tell his two young daughters that their mother, a soldier, has died in Iraq. He decides to put it off as long as possible by taking them to Enchanted Gardens, the Disney World substitute. As the three drive through a landscape of big-box stores, motels, and chain restaurants, we see the beige landscape our soldiers are fighting for in Iraq. The only other recent film I can recall showing this landscape is *The Brown Bunny*, the film in which Chloë Sevigny gives Vincent Gallo a blow job. I don't necessarily recommend pairing them as a double feature.

In Cusack's other wartime effort, the near-future satire *War, Inc.*, he plays a weary corporate hitman going through the motions in a war-torn country named Turaqistan. It's to his credit that Cusack wants to make movies that investigate or indict contemporary reality, but *War, Inc.*'s satire is hesitant and chaste. It gets lost in set pieces that only try to replicate the things they're supposed to be mocking.

A meal Cusack shares with Marisa Tomei (canny

left-wing reporter) and Hilary Duff (whorish Turaqistani pop star) at an abandoned château should have been a Renoiresque highlight, the heart and soul of the film. Here we get the first inkling the trio constitutes some kind of sexually tense family. Instead, it turns into a tribute to the torture scene in *Reservoir Dogs*, which is emerging as the primal scene of all Iraq war-era movies and maybe the entire era in general.

I saw the documentary *The War Tapes* on DVD and made the mistake of watching the bonus features first. One of the bonus features turned out to be résumés for director Deborah Scranton and producer Chuck Lacy. Scranton is a former director of network-TV sports who graduated from Brown with a degree in semiotics. She's also a former member of the US Ski Team who lives on a farm in the mountains of New Hampshire. Lacy, the former president of Ben & Jerry's, runs a venture capital fund and in his spare time breeds grass-fed cattle and imports yerba maté from Paraguay. After I read that I had to take a day off before I watched the film so I could evaluate it without prejudice. Also to reassess my life.

Scranton and Lacy made *The War Tapes* by giving small video cameras to soldiers in a New Hampshire National Guard unit stationed in Iraq in 2004. The film uses footage shot by three of the soldiers: Mike Moriarty, an unemployed forklift operator who would like his kids to see him 'as a good man who was brave'; Steve Pink, an acerbic carpenter whose graphic letters home reveal a good writer; and Zack Bazzi, a serious-minded liberal who moved to the US from Lebanon when he was a child and wants to be career soldier.

All the footage these men shot is riveting, even when it's boring. Sometimes little is going on and the men just horse around or complain about KBR and Halliburton. Then comes the poetry of burning trucks, then sickening incidents. Riding in their Humvee one night, the men strike and kill an Iraqi woman as she's crossing the street carrying a box of cookies. Scranton and Lacy are not content to let the soldiers' footage speak for itself. They add ominous music and turn it into an Iraq-based episode of *Ice Road Truckers*, abusing the pact they seem to have made with these soldiers by giving them cameras.

The three men are inherently interesting, even after they return from the war. Bazzi remains unflappable, opposed to the war but not the military and concerned about the way the media portrays vets as PTSD-addled head cases. Moriarty takes a lot of pain medication for injuries he sustained in Iraq and goes through a couple of jobs before settling down into a good one with the town where he lives. Pink seems bitter about his experiences; he rants about how the war is about money and oil, 'and somebody better get some pretty soon besides Dick Cheney or none of those lives were worth it' – 1,800 soldiers had died when Pink said that and gas cost $2.23 a gallon.

The Ground Truth takes us through the process of joining the army, going to war, and coming home with your face burned off or without your legs. Although this documentary is unapologetic about emphasizing the last part of the process, it doesn't neglect the first part. *The Ground Truth* exposes US Army recruiting as a form of unregulated advertising and Marine Corps recruiting as out-and-out fraud. The film portrays basic training as psychological torture designed to obliterate personality. It shows how new recruits, naturally opposed to taking lives for no reason, learn to enjoy singing songs about killing, with ethnic slurs that make them easier to memorize

Once they were in Iraq, one soldier notes that 'the killing of civilians started to pile up.' Another points out that 'peer-pressure group killing is not necessarily courage.' They are different people when they get home. A 23-year-old veteran hangs himself because he can't stop thinking of himself as a murderer. Another laments, 'Even if I become a Muslim, if I read the Koran every day,' it wouldn't bring back the woman he accidentally killed.

This grim film ends on a heroic note when a soldier named Camilo Mejía decides his conscience won't allow him to return to Iraq for another tour of duty.

Mejía defies the rule that once in the armed forces you must continue to fight in an illegal war. Patricia Foulkrod, the film's director, does not defy the rule that documentaries must include sentimental music, photo montages, and stock footage.

The Situation claims it was the first fiction feature to deal with the war in Iraq. The film is set in Morocco, the pretend Iraq, and features fake Middle Eastern music. The strapping, apple-cheeked Danish actress Connie Nielsen plays a courageous war correspondent caught between two men. In crucial scenes, I was distracted by a large silver ring she wears. *The Situation* has an air of Hollywood glamour and self-congratulation that it tries to efface at every turn. And it's not even a Hollywood film. A couple of lines in the end credits sum up these problems. Special thanks go to Sa Majesté le Roi Mohammed VI, Roi du Maroc and Cynthia Rowley Sunglasses.

The Kingdom is unabashed overkill entertainment. Made during wartime and dealing specifically with the global war on terror, it seems more like a prewar film, straight-up Hollywood action-adventure fantasy from another time. It's far too gruesome for what it wants to be, and too late.

A crack FBI team goes into Saudi Arabia to

investigate the bombing of an American workers' city. Two of the team are mock-squabbling Jennifer Garner and Jason Bateman. Chris Cooper, the senior guy, rubs team leader Jamie Foxx's chest: 'Feels like you got a beast in there.' Later Jeremy Piven feels Foxx's chest, too. This was written by the screenwriter who wrote *Lions for Lambs*, a unique talent. Some of his dialogue, post-bombing: 'My five-year-old boy, when I got home, had a box of Band-Aids and was trying to put his mama's mouth back on.'

Rendition asks us to oppose something everybody is already opposed to, the torture of innocent people. If the Egyptian-American who's whisked away to an unnamed Middle Eastern country (Morocco) to be tortured had in fact been a terrorist, this film might have worked. We would have had to ask ourselves if we were opposed to the torture of viable suspects in the war on terror. But in *Rendition* we get the torture-porn thrill of watching an innocent man be interrogated – blonde Reese Witherspoon's husband, no less – at the same time as we get to deplore that this happens.

Jake Gyllenhaal, an unlikely CIA bureau chief, watches with increasing desperation as interrogation techniques become enhanced. His subplot mirrors *The Devil Wears Prada*. When he finally quits his demeaning job, he throws his cell phone in the water, just like Anne Hathaway did in that movie. Maybe next he goes and gets a job at the *New York Sun* or the *Village Voice* or wherever it was supposed to be.

Even though *Ghosts of Abu Ghraib* came out more than a year before Errol Morris's *Standard Operating Procedure*, which covers the same subject, I saw the Errol Morris film first. It's striking how similar the two films are, not just because they both deal with the torture of prisoners at Abu Ghraib and the scandal that broke when photographs of the abuse appeared in 2004. The main difference between the two films, and this is not to Morris's credit, since *Ghosts of Abu Ghraib* is straightforward, TV-style documentary and not great art like Morris makes, is that *Standard Operating Procedure* is obsessed with infographically investigating the photographs and has Lynndie England in it.

Rory Kennedy's film, more of an exposé than an investigation, is the better of the two. That Morris's film got a theatrical release and Kennedy's premiered on HBO says something about what is deemed worthy of theatrical release in this country, and why. Kennedy's film uses the same techniques as TV news shows, which makes her film more overtly cheesy than Morris's, which, with its barking-dog and creaking-chain reenactments, was also cheesy. But in Kennedy's film we get the sense that she feels these techniques are being put in the service of finding out the truth, whereas in Morris's film we get the sense that he's looking at people like they are bugs, then finding out the truth. They are stand-ins for Bush, Cheney, and Rumsfeld, whose victims they are. It's these higher-ups who are guilty – and here the sound editor cuts in the loud thwack of a rubber stamp – GUILTY! Morris's attitude raises the question of why he doesn't make a film about Bush, Cheney, and Rumsfeld, and of course the answer is that he can't because they would never talk to him. So *Standard Operating Procedure* tortures Lynndie England with Morris's Interrotron camera, using her (and her fellow soldiers) as replacements for the people he'd really like to pin down.

Ghosts of Abu Ghraib takes the visual simile of 'ghost' detainees – detainees brought in off the books so they can be tortured in secret – too far. But so did Morris's film. Why do all American films, even American films made by intelligent documentarians, have to literalize everything? Maybe that has something to do with why Morris used Danny Elfman for his score. We automatically associate Elfman's music with Tim Burton, the great literalizer of childhood imagination. The problem is that scary music – and the music in *Ghosts of Abu Ghraib* is pretty scary – makes too much obvious sense. Abu Ghraib may remind us of certain scenes in *Carrie*, but it is not *Carrie*, it is real, and that's the point. What happened at Abu Ghraib may be the product of a culture formed by Stephen King, but in making films about it, serious filmmakers would do better not to indulge their inner *Cujo*.

Certain people appear as interview subjects in a number of different war-on-terror documentaries – the prison guards from Abu Ghraib, anti-abuse navy men Alberto Mora and John Hutson, legal scholars and authors like Scott Horton and Alfred McCoy, the infamous John Yoo, who is always bland and calm. Their various appearances in these films were shot probably only months apart, but seeing each of them one after another in different films, in different jackets under different lighting, we watch them age before the camera with the strain of telling their stories again. Meanwhile, we see the same clips of George W. Bush saying he's going to 'smoke 'em out and get 'em runnin',' or Donald Rumsfeld saying he was only kidding about standing up eight to ten hours a day. They are frozen in those moments when they appear stupid and evil, yet these clips take them out of life and into some timeless realm of official TV where no one is ever punished. Maybe punishment is what happens on home video, then on YouTube, like it did to Saddam Hussein.

If, by July 2007, you had not heard there was a war going on in Iraq, then *No End in Sight* was the documentary for you. The film had a real audience of maybe two people – two people, by the way, I would be happy to meet. The film is meticulous in establishing that the war was a botched job from the beginning, and it gets a lot of well-known people to appear on camera to support that extremely noncontroversial viewpoint. Then it concludes that, since American soldiers have died in this war or were horribly maimed or crippled for life, we have got to find something good about it. It is easy to get confused and emotional when you are dealing with veterans whose lives have been permanently altered for the worse, but you've got to figure things out a little more than that before you make a movie.

A documentary from the early 1980s called *The Atomic Cafe* changed everything. It introduced the idea that history could be told via stock-footage orgy, a fun combination of clips strung together for maximum hilarity at the expense of the people who shot them. Industrial films, TV commercials, military films, TV news footage, scenes from B movies, home movies – detritus from the lower rungs of film history could be marshaled into formation to make glib points about things we are against.

Most documentaries do this now, even if that's not all they do. So for instance in *Why We Fight*, a documentary on the militarization of our culture and how that led to the war on terror, if the narrator mentions 'cities' and 'work' we are treated to sixty-year-old stock footage of people flooding into the lobbies of office buildings.

What we are seeing when this happens is America's Greatest Hits, an exercise in nostalgia that shows up our era in favor of a time when the average person dressed a little better and his most cherished goal was not to grow up to be Jimmy Fallon. This is lazy film-making, but it can be pretty entertaining. In *Why We Fight*, we get to see a Halliburton promotional film from 1951 in which the original narrator chirps, 'There she is – oil! That's what all the fuss is about.'

One of America's Greatest Hits was President Dwight Eisenhower's farewell address, which he delivered live from the Oval Office on January 17, 1961. The former general warned the country about the creeping influence of what he called the military-industrial complex. The country, the film notes, didn't listen. Of course we don't see the whole speech – that would be boring. Instead, we get to see bits of it Photoshopped into TV screens in stock footage of 1950s living rooms. As Oliver North once said: *Neat!*

It's not that *Why We Fight* is wrong. It's a collage, but it's not wrong. No, it invites us to contemplate its rightness even as it contemplates its rightness itself. Given the subject matter, it does that in a pretty serene way. It demonstrates that there is no point of radicalism from which it could do anything else. So 'why we fight' also means 'why we don't fight,' why we are passive, why we don't rebel.

Today people are very concerned about where their food comes from. They want to know that the ingredients in it are fresh, organic, locally grown, all that stuff. That's how I feel about documentaries. Where did all this footage come from? Wouldn't it be better if the director made it all himself? Or maybe making films like this is like making your house out of straw, sticks, and brick, and then putting aluminum siding on it and columns out front. Funny, yes. A little scary. I wouldn't want to live there.

Taxi to the Dark Side overwhelms you with detail so repellent and frightening that by the end of it you are fully convinced that no punishment could be painful enough for the Bush administration. The film calls them murderers and makes the charge stick. It too often relies on ominosity (the American cinema has become an ominosity machine) but the depth of the information presented here excuses the film's excess. Who knew Guantánamo Bay had a gift shop where you could buy T-shirts that say GUANTANAMO BAY BEHAVIOR MODIFICATION INSTRUCTOR CUBA? Who knew the enhanced interrogation techniques used there included forcing detainees to wear pointed birthday hats? Alex Gibney, the film's director, covers his subject more thoroughly than any book or article I've read. It is without question the grimmest film on the war, and that's saying something.

It's best, however, when it sticks to its main story, essentially an onscreen autopsy. Dilawar was a taxi driver who was stopped by Afghan warlords in December 2002 and turned over to US forces for money. Chained in the prison at Bagram, he was beaten for days until he died. His legs were so 'pulpified' by the beatings that had he lived it would've been necessary to amputate them. His guards beat him so he'd shut up because he was screaming in pain and continued beating him after he'd died because they thought he was faking immobility. They jumped on his back until they were tired, took breaks, then beat him some more. He was shackled the whole time. Dilawar didn't have a last name but back in his village he got one on his gravestone: THE MARTYR.

Gibney traces these techniques up through the chain of command, where Donald Rumsfeld stands all day and tells reporters 'life goes on.' A lieutenant general explains enhanced interrogation techniques, inadvertently describing the war on terror at the same time: 'It was California avocado freestyle. I mean, it was just a free-for-all.'

Iraq in Fragments is so good I'm surprised people even recognize it as a movie. It's devoid of the clutter other documentaries rely on for visual interest. (Most documentaries are radio with pictures.) The person who made it, James Longley, also shot it, recorded the sound, and edited it. His cinematography is so superior to the cinematography in any of these other documentaries that he must be a Martian. Longley made his film in Iraq, not in a TV studio or in Morocco. He does not have to thank Sa Majesté or Cynthia Rowley for anything. The film's stars are the Mahdi Army and the people of Baghdad and Kurdistan.

If only for the way the movie reveals Iraq as a country of colors instead of just the tan dust we see in other Iraq war movies, this film would be exceptional. These vibrant images switch between the tranquil – fruit and vegetables for sale in a market, fish in an aquarium – and the violent – the scarves covering the faces of the Mahdi Army vigilantes kicking the alcohol sellers, the strings of colored lights lining the streets at night as flagellants parade by, beating themselves with metal chains.

Longley lets things play out, even speeches and the harangues of clerics. The sound in the film is unlike that in other films, too. Longley makes sure the sound always works in tandem with the images to evoke the places where they were shot, not to explain them. In the film's final third, shot in Kurdistan, where the sky is full of smoke from brick kilns and the fields are covered with sunflowers, Longley's filmmaking pares things down to an elemental level reminiscent of Dovzhenko: images of fire, the moon, snow, bones, and blood. The film ends in twilight with a Kurd reminding us that 'nobody can escape America's reach' and that when it's all over, the winners always let you know God was on their side.

Brian De Palma's *Redacted* aroused controversy when it came out in late 2007, the kind of ridiculous controversy that is the hallmark of our time. The film found no audience and played on few screens, but the right-wing media howled.

Bill O'Reilly and others called for De Palma and the film's producer, TV and sports magnate Mark Cuban, to be arrested for treason and sued for defamation. In an attempt to hit them where they live, right-wingers demanded fans boycott the Dallas Mavericks, one of Cuban's properties. Later it emerged that Cuban had in fact cut the film's final scenes, fearing they would cause 'emotional distress' and result in lawsuits from the families of real soldiers. TV personalities getting together to decry a basketball team because of a movie that's already been expurgated by its producer – we don't have censorship in this country, we have synergy.

Redacted fictionalizes the Mahmudiyah rampage, in which five American infantrymen gang-raped and murdered a 14-year-old Iraqi girl after killing her parents and her sister, a toddler. De Palma goes for a new kind of annoying realism by showing this played out in various media, including the ones that went on to attack him, yet at the same time *Redacted* feels stagy. The film is a clunky combination of De Palma's Vietnam movie *Casualties of War* and the amazing 'Be Black, Baby' section of his underrated *Hi, Mom!* For a film of such urgency, *Redacted* is inferior to the De Palma movie that preceded it, the trashy *Black Dahlia*, also a fictionalized account of an infamous real-life rape and murder.

Shot in Jordan, not Morocco, *Redacted* moved in the direction of Iraq, not Hollywood. *Battle for Haditha*, also the reenactment of a war atrocity, also shot in Jordan, moves even closer. Improvised around the story of how marines murdered twenty-four innocent Iraqi men, women, and children in al-Anbar province in November 2005, *Battle for Haditha* is the best Iraq combat film yet made, which is to say the only good one.

The British director Nick Broomfield, known in this country for documentaries like *Kurt & Courtney* and *Biggie and Tupac*, interlaces three stories in a way that owes more to neorealism than 'hyperlink' cinema, that already forgotten term for movies like *Syriana* and *Babel*. Broomfield presents a middle-aged ex-Baathist, the insurgent who plants an IED that leads to the bloodbath, as an irked, confused speechifier without reducing him to pure villain status. I didn't get the name of the actor who plays this difficult, thankless role. The names of Arab actors are too easily buried and forgotten, like the names of the Arab dead. Elliot Ruiz's portrait of a competent, intelligent 20-year-old soldier who is nonetheless guilty of murder is flawless. To successfully improvise a part this grueling without going over the top is a sign of real distinction.

A throwaway scene in *Battle for Haditha* sticks in my mind: a marine forced to drop and do push-ups while chanting 'I will not be funny anymore.' For me, this quick scene encapsulates something real that it's glib to acknowledge: the war on terror is one group of Americans punishing another for the 1990s – in another country, with lots of collateral damage.

You can shoot a reenactment feature where it took place, even if it took place in Pakistan and Afghanistan. But what if part of it took place in the prison cells and interrogation rooms of the Guantánamo Bay detention facility? Michael Winterbottom and Mat Whitecross, British directors like Nick Broomfield, knew they would not be allowed to film in Camp X-Ray and Camp Delta, so they re-created the Guantánamo center in a hospitable country near where they were already shooting: Iran.

The Road to Guantánamo, one of the essential war-on-terror films, begins unpromisingly as extreme-travel TV or the first episode of *Real World: Guantánamo Bay*. We meet the Tipton Three (although they are not called that in the film), young British men of Pakistani decent who were kidnapped by the United Front in Afghanistan. Quickly the film shifts tone, the story becomes more and more harrowing as the photography of landscapes and faces becomes more beautiful. Thoughts of *Harold & Kumar Escape from*

Guantánamo Bay dissipate well before the three (now played by actors) are trapped inside a truck that's filling up with blood as dozens of prisoners scramble over each other to avoid the bullets Afghani soldiers shoot through its walls.

Once in Cuba, the three are subjected to abuse that includes the nonstop yelling of their fascistic American guards, whose evident fear of being looked at tends to impart demonic power to the boys' collective gaze. 'Don't let 'em look!' and 'Face away from us!' are the commands of powerless people who are afraid to be seen because they know what they're doing is wrong. Two years later, the guards still harangue them as they are driven by bus past the HONOR BOUND TO DEFEND FREEDOM sign and taken out of the prison camp to be set free: 'Don't look out the window!' The film makes those five words as sickening as anything that's happened in the war on terror.

In 1981, the English band Au Pairs had a song called 'Armagh,' about an Irish woman tortured in a British prison. The first lines went:

> We don't torture, we're a civilized nation.
> We're avoiding any confrontation.

Is their country's experience in Northern Ireland the reason British filmmakers are making better films about the war on terror than Americans?

Maybe. But right after *The Road to Guantánamo*, Michael Winterbottom, without Mat Whitecross, made *A Mighty Heart*, from Mariane Pearl's book about the kidnapping and murder of her husband, the journalist Daniel Pearl, by terrorist jihadis in Pakistan in early 2002. Shot in Pakistan and India, the film strives for the kind of grainy shaky-cam realism on which *The Road to Guantánamo* did not rely.

A Mighty Heart stars Angelina Jolie as Mariane Pearl. The first half of the movie is like a documentary about Jolie playing Mariane, the reenactment of a reenactment like *The Road to Guantánamo*. We watch her acting, she walks around with a prosthetic pregnant belly, under-plays her phone reaction to Daniel's boneheaded parents, who think everything is going to work out fine. The third quarter of *A Mighty Heart* is a very good episode of *Karachi Vice* – 'I love this town,' an American intelligence agent exclaims. The last quarter is back to Jolie. Her lower lip is dry, later almost split, illustrating the film's arc of emotional destitution.

Mostly she's on the phone. Not just her; everyone in *A Mighty Heart* is on the phone. The film is an investigation into cell phone use among Westerners who live in big houses in Karachi; it's a film about manners. The cell phone is the instrument the Westerners use to control the world around them, a world where they make everyone their servant. Even when Daniel is out working, his nice-guy unctuousness gives him away as a privileged Westerner. He might as well be ordering organic pizza in a restaurant in Brooklyn. He's always all 'Yeah, no, I'm good' and 'I'm gonna let you go, OK?' Still, he depends on his cell phone less than the others, and the film implies he's punished for it. When he's kidnapped, Mariane loses phone contact with him, a sign of grave danger. In bed at night, with little hope, she continues to send texts he'll never read: 'I love you.'

What Winterbottom intended is unclear. He does the best he can under the circumstances, working with the biggest star in the world to help her tell the most important story on earth, ambiguously undercutting it with repetitive actions showing Americans as both all-powerful and ineffectual. Were the Pearls really like this? By the film's end, after Mariane gives birth, we see her and her child as a unit complete without Daniel. Wistful music from the band Nouvelle Vague plays. Is this supposed to be melancholy, or is it a testament to the superfluousness of the Western male, or both?

A Mighty Heart ends with a birth, *The Hills Have Eyes II* starts with one. A cinematic coincidence, but maybe it's in trash like this that we'll find the truth of the situation. After all, it's the torture porn of the *Hostel* and *Saw* franchises, made concurrently with the prisoner abuse at Abu Ghraib, that exposed certain truths about American culture before the Abu Ghraib photos did.

Even better, *The Hills Have Eyes II* is explicitly a war film. National Guard troops on a training exercise in the New Mexico desert, which we're initially led to think is Afghanistan or Iraq, run around yelling 'America number one, bitch!' Soon they begin to get picked off Indian-style by relatives of the mutant family from the first remake of *The Hills Have Eyes*. This is a promising start, but the movie ends up being less effective than it should be. Too bad producer Wes Craven assigned it to a director of videos for Nickelback and Sisqo when it needed a John Carpenter. One gory image lingers, a dead guy with his wallet shoved into his head.

Wouldn't it be funny if it turned out that World Wrestling Entertainment had made one of the best films about the war in Iraq? That's the kind of dumb hope I had going into *The Marine*. John Cena, the professional wrestler, a bulky Matt Damon delivered by forceps, plays the title role, a veteran of the war in Iraq. Returning to his blonde wife in South Carolina, he finds the only job he can get is security guard. After he's fired for throwing somebody through a plate-glass window, he goes home and confesses his biggest fear: sitting around at home doing nothing.

Triton (that's the marine's last name) is like the United States. He's never learned that all men's miseries come from not being able to sit quietly in a room alone. The couple decides to take a road trip in their Lincoln Navigator, a preposterous vehicle for them to own, but I guess not more than it is for anybody else. A gas station blows up, Triton's wife is kidnapped – significantly, he is robbed at a gas pump. Now Triton is back in his element, once again doing what he was trained to do in Iraq. For the rest of the movie he is shot at thousands and thousands of times and not hit once.

With the exception of trash movies, war-on-terror films are so grim, dismal, and tragic that when you have contempt for one, you feel bad about it. *Gunner Palace*, a documentary in the form of a music video, promotes the war in Iraq as crazy fucked-up shit that nobody but the grunts and a few haji good guys understand – and the film's director, who narrates in a cool-guy whisper that sounds like he's auditioning to dub *Two or Three Things I Know About Her* into English.

Right off, this sub-Godardian voice-over is childish and filled with hokey attitude. 'Most of us don't see this on the news anymore. We have reality TV instead – *Joe Millionaire*, *Survivor*. Well, survive this: a year in Baghdad without changing the channel.' When the filmmaker tells us, 'Unlike a movie, war has no end,' we don't bother to sort that out because we are glad that at least movies have an end. In a piece from 1955 on Soviet films, Robert Warshow wrote that 'the commentator is one of the diseases of our time and must be endured; he will be there at the end of the world to say into a microphone: 'This is the end of the world." But Warshow didn't know the commentator would be hip.

Making a film this bad helps no one. It's also inappropriately lame. When a soldier shows an Iraqi orphan a SpongeBob SquarePants doll, a title appears over the image: SPONGEBOB. The film becomes human when the soldiers *Gunner Palace* follows around are allowed to speak for themselves. The hilarious slacker SPC Stuart Wilf tells us that it's better to be in Iraq than to be a loser in his hometown, where he'd be doing nothing because there's nothing to do. This 19-year-old combat veteran speaks for everyone who's from a place like that, and the sanity of his position is only bolstered by the way he dances around in a Saudi robe he bought on leave in Qatar. Wilf comes across as all-American and a total fuckup, a much more appealing figure than John Cena's ludicrous marine, and more heroic.

Kimberley Peirce's 1999 feature debut, *Boys Don't Cry*, was as assured and fully achieved as Nicholas Ray's debut was fifty years earlier. Like *They Live by Night*, *Boys Don't Cry* showed a flair for drama that was intimate but explosive, and had a true understanding for the pain outsiders feel in love. Why, then, nine years later, is Peirce imitating *Gunner Palace*? *Stop-Loss* had the potential to be the best movie about the war in Iraq. The combat scenes early in the film are the best-directed combat scenes in any war-on-terror movie. When they end, *Stop-Loss* resorts to an MTV-inspired version of media realism – soldiers' video diary footage and interludes of rap – that has nothing to do with the story Peirce wants to tell, and has everything to do with keeping the attention of her perceived audience so she can tell them an important story. The film has to jerk itself out of this mode whenever it wants to be a film at all.

When actor-director Liev Schreiber and his producer on *Everything Is Illuminated*, an adaptation of the Jonathan Safran Foer novel, go to the airport to pick up an intern coming to work on their film, we are witnessing not just a historic first in the history of interning but also the beginning of one of the best movies about the war on terror. Nina Davenport's documentary *Operation Filmmaker* is only tangentially related to the actual war in Iraq, but it has more to say about the issues animating it than most films dealing with it directly.

Having seen a young Iraqi film student named Muthana Mohmed interviewed in Baghdad by MTV, Schreiber gets the genius idea to hire Muthana and fly him to Prague, where Schreiber's film is shooting.

Soon Muthana, the Stuart Wilf of international film production, is charged with tasks like mixing vegan snacks in little plastic cups for producers who must constantly be treated like babies. Producer Peter Saraf, unhappy with the slacker Muthana's attitude, schools him: Muthana has to learn to make himself invaluable to his bosses. He must fawn over his producer and director. For instance, to ingratiate himself, he should bring them coffee in the middle of meetings – but discreetly and quietly. That's how we do it in America, Saraf explains. Nothing demeaning about it. Totally normal. We all came up that way.

A better portrait of how people who think of themselves as Good turn the disadvantaged into their slaves has never been put on film. *Operation Filmmaker*, the entire thing a subtle metaphor for the way America helps Iraq by occupying it, damns everyone it touches, including Muthana and the filmmaker herself. After Muthana expresses his admiration for George W. Bush, the producers of *Everything Is Illuminated* pretty much abandon him to fend for himself. He stays in Prague, gets a job on a movie based on the video game *Doom*, and convinces its affable star, Dwayne 'The Rock' Johnson, to pay for him to go to film school in London. The Rock may have been conned by Muthana, but why should he care? The Rock's a movie star, he's got money, and he can give it out any way he chooses. In *Operation Filmmaker* a professional wrestler really does come to the rescue, and Davenport has the grace not to make the ironic but obvious point that the Rock is a Republican and Saraf and Schreiber are Democrats.

Maybe in movies right now the war is best approached obliquely. *Full Battle Rattle*, by Tony Gerber and Jesse Moss, documents what happens at the National Training Center at Fort Irwin, a thousand-mile tract of the Mojave Desert comprising thirteen replica Iraqi villages. The army sees this as a stage set where soldiers learn how to handle themselves in the real theater of war. A Lieutenant Colonel McLoughlin, training there, explains: 'Our number one priority is to provide hope to the people. All our bright thinking here is all for naught if we don't control the crowd.'

These soldiers learn to control the crowd by playing cowboys and Indians in a landscape where Indians used to be. The center employs 250 Arabic-speaking Iraqi-Americans, who are given character biographies and scripts so they can portray townspeople, insurgents, and Iraqi policemen. In one scenario, the son of the deputy mayor is accidentally killed by American firepower. Negotiations begin that are more like *The Price Is Right* than a war movie. American soldiers carry around $2,500 in play money to pay off relatives of the dead. Then the brass steps in for further smoothing, awkwardly rehearsing for the real thing. 'I have a contract for a sewage system,' says Lt. Col. McLoughlin.

'It's worth over $280,000 – approved!' He seals the deal: 'Have some fruit. This is our best fruit.'

It's not just the soldiers who believe in this fiction the army's created. The middle-aged Iraqi man who plays the deputy mayor longs to be promoted to the status of full mayor. At work in the Mojave his dignity is restored. Later we see him at his other job, manning the cash register at a liquor store in a desolate San Diego neighborhood.

This beautifully composed documentary provides the most human and balanced view in any of these films. It's a hopeful, even utopian film that takes place far away from the Green Zone and Abu Ghraib, strangely touching and sad. A doctor shows us mannequin limbs with carved plastic wounds. 'These injuries are exact replicas,' he says. The limbs snap back into place. By the time the film was done, five of the soldiers in it were already dead.

Dick Cheney has told us this war will not end in our lifetime. An era of endless war chokes off the kind of evaluation that in the past has produced the best war movies. If the war on terror never ends, those films cannot be made. Evaluation will be left to movies like *The Dark Knight*, which indulge our longing for relief from war at the same time as they replicate its stasis and reconfigure its atrocities as blockbuster entertainment.

You always hear conservatives say Hollywood hates America. To me, what proves Hollywood hates America is the way they keep making Batman movies. Meanwhile, no Hollywood filmmakers have gone to Iraq. All the 1990s World War II films Hollywood made, the *Saving Private Ryan*s, with their Pentagon advisers and Department of Defense equipment they got at the cost of script approval, were made by people pretending they wanted to go to war. *If only we had a war*, they seemed to moan. *Ach, we were born too late!*

Here was your chance, Hollywood, to emulate the Greatest Generation filmmakers you professed to admire so much. What you made instead were things like *War of the Worlds*, a film that reveled in the destruction of New York, then hightailed it through the woods to grandmother's house. Sleep tight.

[2007]

Molly Young

– Kickstart My Heart –

Among children born in America in the late 1980s, my classmates at the San Francisco Day School must have been the happiest, healthiest, most unthinkingest cluster of them all. Our parents raised us to give thoughtful Bar Mitzvah gifts, walk or jog daily, recognize Kwanzaa. If the community was not quite anti-intellectual, it was certainly not a culture of quiet indoor pursuits. The weather was too nice, for one thing. And our parents, who hadn't attended Ivy League schools and didn't read literature, had yet done well enough to afford beach houses up the coast and a rainbow flock of Polar Fleeces. Among us, their off-spring, there was no such thing as academic rivalry. We worked together if we worked at all.

This changed when I began my first year at the Ivy League university where I am now a senior. Here I met freshmen who had taken the SATs more than twice, who spoke three Asian languages, who began drinking coffee in middle school. 'Things are different on the East Coast,' I told my mother on a cellphone from the campus Starbucks, where I was conspicuously reading the *New Yorker* and hoping to make friends. The kids of the East Coast intellectual guard had a whole culture of rituals and objectives by which to define themselves: anticipation of the LSATs, the *New Criterion,* cocaine.

It was this New York and Boston-bred clique that taught me what I know about Adderall – or showed me, rather, since the drug is less talked about than exhibited. It is not hard to tell if someone has taken a lot of Adderall. His mouth will be tensed, his shoulders stiff, his gaze unwavering. Everyone looks the same after ten or so hours of untrammeled focus. During freshman year I got mine from Bronson, a sloth of a boy from Brooklyn whom I hooked up with at a party. Bronson was prescribed the drug for his ADD but it had a somewhat deadening effect on him, and he made extra cash by selling what he didn't use or want. Once a month I would visit him to sit on his dorm bed while he counted out pills from an organizer. There was a *Scarface* poster on the wall and a jar of weed on the mini-fridge, which Bronson would uncap and wave under my nose, as though it were single-malt scotch or chloroform. He refused to sell me his 20-milligram pills because he thought I might have a heart attack, so I took 10s.

Adderall comes in two forms: fast-acting and extended release. Fast-acting looks like aspirin and has a sweetish taste. In theory it can be be crushed and snorted, though I've never seen anyone cut a line of Adderall purely for recreation. Bronson sold me the extended release version, marketed as Adderall XR, which resembles something that Neely would have chased with vodka in *Valley of the Dolls.* It is the Las Vegas of pills, an object that conforms so gleefully to every pill cliché that taking it feels cinematic. The drug comes in a gleaming capsule, blue or tangerine colored, and it can be swallowed or sprinkled over cafeteria applesauce. It is made of equal portions of four amphetamines, all of which the body metabolizes at different rates, and which are packaged in tiny rotund beads that dissolve at varied speeds, so the effect is consistent. A 10-milligram capsule lasts about six hours and a 20-milligram capsule doubles the duration.

It is difficult to know whether it is a drug itself or a drug culture that attracts certain people to certain substances. In the case of Adderall, I came for the culture and stayed for the drug. Nothing had ever tempted me before. As an adolescent girl, alcohol was closely allied with promiscuity, and I was a prude. Weed suggested foolishness and snacking, and I was foolish and hungry enough as it was. But then came college, and with it, Adderall – a drug associated with writing, thinking, and joyful, hermetic reading. Adderall Me and Ideal Me were nearly the same person, and I saw no reason not to dabble in my best self.

Adderall has been on the market since 1996. It is produced by the British drug maker Shire Pharmaceuticals, and is currently the 125th most popular clinical drug in America. The Shire website offers some vague information about ADHD, the disorder for which Adderall is prescribed, and warns that the consequences of untreated ADHD can include relationship problems, drug abuse, and frequent job changes. There is a link for people who are already taking Adderall. 'Congratulations!' it reads. 'By taking ADDERALL XR, you're showing your commitment to reaching your potential in all aspects of your life – and to being the person you were meant to be.'

Once or twice a week during my first three years of college I'd dip into my supply of pills (I kept them in a turquoise Tiffany's case, to avoid crushing), gather a bundle of work, and incubate myself in the common room of the French House, where I lived. I had to be careful not to take the drug in my dorm room, because if I did, I might spend hours plucking my eyebrows or digitally altering photographs. The common room was a ballroom-sized space with a fireplace, wood paneling, velvet chairs, and a desk. It was a popular place to work among my housemates, but I liked to work alone in my Adderall outfit (a t-shirt with the armpits stained corncob-yellow from amphetamine sweat), so I would push all the furniture except one chair into an adjacent room and shut the doors. There were water fountains nearby and nobody bothered me.

The feeling begins about twenty minutes after you take the pill: a mental tightening, as though someone had refined your scope of vision into a narrow and penetrating line. All peripheral distractions disappear (you would make a very poor hunter or soccer player). There is a slight fluttering of the heart, and gentle, persistent waves of warmth that are not distracting unless it is hot outside. This is how I experienced Adderall; some people have panic attacks and others feel nothing at all.

Any actual amount of time spent under the influence is hard to describe, because time passes very quickly. It's a euphoric drug, but also an alienating one. If I took a pill with my morning coffee, it would wear off by early evening. All of my work for the coming week would be finished, and I could take an aspirin, shower, and go to bed. Having missed the transition from day to night as well as all three meals, my dreams would be hysterical, but I always woke the next day feeling chipper and accomplished.

Faking ADHD is a cakewalk, but the testing process is expensive. It is easier to buy the drug from those who already have it, for $2 a pill, or $3, or $5 if you are dim enough to make your purchase during finals period. The summer after sophomore year, stranded without Bronson and determined to write a novel, I found an online foreign pharmacy that sent encrypted catalogs of drugs to my Gmail account. Rohypnol, Valium, Oxycodone, Prozac, and Ritalin were all in stock

– no Adderall, but Ritalin would do in a pinch. (Ritalin is the Salieri to Adderall's Mozart.) I bought thirty tabs of generic Ritalin with a moneygram. It cost fifty dollars, but I was living at home that summer, and also, I reasoned, I'd save money on all the food I wouldn't eat.

'Who do you know in Panama City?' my mom asked when the package arrived. Inside was a folder wrapped in black sandpaper and a 'Smints container full of pills. The Ritalin lasted all summer, and in September I traded the leftovers for Adderall. When I ran out and couldn't locate any more at school (Bronson was abroad), I called a friend at Sarah Lawrence, who sent me envelopes of pills wrapped in tissue paper.

Like so many things at my school, Adderall consumption has a lot to do with money. One senses that the students who blow $100 a month on extended release capsules are the same ones buying prosciutto sandwiches for lunch instead of eating in the cafeteria. But unlike other drugs, Adderall doesn't lend itself to group consumption, so it is hard to tell who does it and how often. Adderall has no Kurt Cobain, no Snoop Dogg or Bret Easton Ellis. It not as glamorous as heroin nor as benign as weed, and it is not a status symbol like cocaine. Adderall, after all, is a drug prescribed to kids who drop their pants in the schoolyard instead of playing hopscotch.

It is probably surprising that the drug backfired only once, when I stayed up on Adderall for 72 hours before a philosophy final. My appearance in the testing hall the next day was so tangled and shaky that the professor removed me from the room. I was sent away with permission to return later and finish the exam in his office. Instead, I slept. In the end it didn't matter that I failed the exam, because a semester of A+ Adderall papers had left me with a decent grade in the class. If the proof is in the transcript, then Adderall is hardly a self-punishing habit. Sometimes I think about how Marion Jones has to return all the prize money she earned while taking steroids, and I wonder whether I should be stripped of all the A's I received for papers written on Adderall. This is a haunting or a comical thought, depending on my mood.

Of course, I could have studied in college without Adderall, just like I did in high school – I just couldn't have studied with such ecstasy. Theoretical texts, in particular, were transformed into exercises as conquerable as a Tuesday crossword. I could work out in the gym with a Xeroxed packet of Gayatri Spivak perched on the elliptical machine in front of me, reading and burning calories at the same time. The efficacy of the multitasking was exhilarating. On Adderall, the densest writing became penetrable. I had an illusion of mastery, at least, that lasted long enough to write the necessary papers and presentations. I could never remember what I had written the next day, but I justified this forgetfulness as an accelerated version of what would happen anyway after I graduated.

More than anything, Adderall simulated the enthusiasm that a good teacher naturally stokes. For three years my brain, normally so recalcitrant, became my will's devoted vehicle. But there's a downside to a drug that makes everything interesting. By the end of junior year, I still had no idea what I liked or was good at. This past fall, when my senior year started, I took a break from the drug – at first because I couldn't find any, and then because I refused it. It took these four abstinent months to realize that I was not supposed to be electrified by everything I learned in school; that some of it had a vaccinating purpose, so that by trying a little now and reacting badly, I could fend it off later.

Finals period without Adderall passed slowly and pleasantly. It turns out that the feverish moral imperative to work was an effect of the drug, not a cause. I lingered over my reading and drank coffee to stay awake. There were no more ecstatic Joan-of-Arc-in-the-library experiences, no more imagined channeling of dead literary critics – but this, I suppose, is appropriate when what's at stake is only a 15-page essay on Jane Austen, double spaced. I turned in my last exam on a snowy Saturday morning and flew home the same day. It was 27 degrees in Boston when I left and 60 in San Francisco when I landed, warm enough to jog without a Polar Fleece.

[2008]

Lawrence Jackson

– Slickheads –

Around my way we really tripped over two things: the beef with them Woodlawn whores in '85; then four years later, when stick-up boys shot Sonny.

In high school, me, Charm Sawyer, and Piccolo Breaks got up a social club called the Oxfords. More or less just the little guys with round glasses from our block, plus an off-brand or two from the Avenue – North or Wabash – or from the Heights – Liberty or Park.

I pimped in the fine honey from church to the jam. Tanya, Carla, Kim, Lisa, Stacy, all of them dying to get out of the house. I was about 15 when I booked out, and it took every bit of two years to get snug. But it had started in middle school with me and Rodney Glide freaking the white girl in the basement and him working her skirt up.

I wasn't really built like that. Check it out. Back in the day I loaded dirt and wood chips at a garden supply store on Wabash. One time, a church girl gave me a ride home after work and I told her wait while I caught a quick shower. Since the old-school play was to answer the Jehovah Witness knock at the door in a towel, any girl at your house was supposed to get open-fly treatment. Church girl called her mother telling her why she was hold up. Her old mother, an ex-opera contralto, started fussing. 'Kim, use common sense. Even little Lair's trying to get some!' I took it as a compliment. Her mother didn't think I was gay the way her unafraid daughter did when I stepped from the shower, still in a towel. That's when I started liking older women, because they always act like, given the chance, you might knock them down. And I got it backwards, since all what she said really did was start me on eating out.

The Oxford clique came together for an obvious reason. When we still footed it to parties and up Rhythm Skate, we needed a whole crew or a connect to get by in the world of yo boys and slickheads. As time went on, the Oxfords put it together for real. Even though all us from out the row house – a snatch of grass in front and the #51 bus chugging by, floods and bugs in the basement, alleyways of blackness out back – all us little men had turned out the next Timex Social Club.

Woodlawn niggers called us the Pajama Crew for spite, because we draped our fathers' old trench coats, that winter of '85. Them County slickheads wore tight their Adidas nylon sweat suits, silk BVDs, and herringbone gold chains, flexing power. But the real Oxford contribution to the B-More scene was the DC Go-Go haircut – the flattop – or sometimes just faded, Jerseyed, Phillied. Bear in mind that your average yo boy from off the corner cut his naps down to the scalp. That's why we called them unremarkable niggers slick-heads.

To me, slickheads lacked imagination, and their haircut was only the beginning of that emptiness. When I was first learning about it, slickhead behavior seemed inhibited, closed down, and reactionary. Like when I was prancing at the Harbor with my merry-go-round honey Sade, me ragging in a cycling cap, moccasins, bleached jeans, and an Ocean Pacific tee of a man surfing on a beach I had never seen, and some slickhead called to her, 'A yo, drop that Prep and get with this Slick.' They had no class, and if I hadn't thought he would have shot me I might have banged him in his mouth. Then again, he wasn't talking to me, and I was into women's lib, eating out and everything.

The Oxfords went for exhibition and fullness, the whole way, and took it straight to those break-dancing older slickhead clowns from Woodlawn. Yeah, they was popping and breaking, helicopter and all that, but that shit is for tourists. Our thing was the leg dances, speeded-up jigs. I copped our step from this old head who rocked coach's shorts and a touring cap, and who gave up the flow downtown every summer. At the Inner Harbor, near the water-taxi line, seven or eight of us would break into the Oxford Bop, a crisscross reel, while we shouted the lyrics to Status IV's 'You Ain't Really Down.'

'Said you were my lady . . . And your love was true . . . !'

More attention than pulling your thing out.

The Oxfords liked a Roman holiday. Pretty Ricky brother crashed through the top of the telephone booth at the Harbor. Charm jumped from the second-floor balcony onto the reception desk in the Comfort Inn lobby. James Brown leapt through a car windshield, hind parts first.

But mainly we threw cranking jams and released our boredom into the laps of the Oxford Pearls. All them was getting down, especially the girls from Catholic school. Even though we modeled ourselves on the oldtime Negro fraternities, chanting 'O-X!' through dim basement corridors pulsating with Chip E. Inc. stutter-singing 'Like This,' the Oxfords could also function like that – like a gang. Coming up in 21215 – Bodymore, Murderland – attending public schools, we only did what we had to do. Anyway, a homeboy of a homeboy kicked some slickhead in the chest over a girl at a high school party at a fraternity house on Liberty Heights, and the war against Woodlawn jumped off.

The jam was a cranker, Darrin Ebron spinning 'Al Naafiysh,' 'Set It Off,' and 'Din Da Da' over and over; naturally it was honey heaven. I was wedging my knees between so many willing thighs that I never saw

Pretty Ricky cousin Jerome and Ron J guff. First thing I knew the music cut off and Pretty Ricky and Mighty Joe Young were shuttling back and forth from the Kappa House to the phone booth in the 7-Eleven parking lot and Charm Sawyer was popping cash shit. I looked out into the mild May night, and it was enough shell-toes and silk BVDs to stop four lanes of traffic. Me and my homeboys were wearing moccasins and corduroy shorts. I had a pound of Dax in my hair, dripping like Shabba-Doo's, but faded like a prep's.

I loaded all of my men into the car and left the scrum thinking I was just helping out, like Jesus would do. I had a Monte Carlo, an orange EXP, an IROC-Z, and a Cressida on my ass – a slickhead caravan in hot pursuit. Then I thought I got lucky.

Northwest Baltimore's finest had been called about the scrap and I braked when the blue lights spun behind me. I pulled over and I told the police everything I knew, which was that some grown men were following me and I was scared. But you know how Five-O handled his bit.

'I want you out my jurisdiction! Get your ass out of my sight!'

You know how Five-O cuss you when he through with you. Then he drove off.

It was six of us in the AMC Sportabout, a car about as good for driving as open-toed shoes for running ball. Besides the fact that the starter on my people's car was iffy, the windows didn't operate, and the door handle on the driver's side was broke. That night I put that old yellow wagon to the test. I headed down Liberty Heights back to Garrison Boulevard, and I learned what Pretty Ricky had been doing on the telephone. He had reached out to his wild cousins, some hoppers who ain't mind popping tool. I took Garrison and that baby right turn by the firehouse to Chelsea Terrace, to fetch some gun-slinging boy from out his house. After Five-O shammed on me, I was needing Ricky's cousin to appear with that .357 Magnum that Hawk carried on *Spenser: For Hire*. Instead a jive compact cat hopped into the old station wagon with barely a .25 in his dip.

Now, I had seen some young boys around my way with tool. I think one of them even got into *Time* for showing up strapped at Garrison or Pimlico, the local junior high schools. In fact, it had been the cats from my year at middle school, the twins from Whitelock Street now going up Walbrook with Charm, who had brought tool to #66, setting the trend right at the beginning of the 1980s. They had got put out for a couple of days for that stunt. The next year, at Harlem Park Middle, them boys had burned up a cat for his Sixers jacket. I had seen a couple niggers pulled off of a public bus and beaten before. I held my ground standing next to a boy from Cherry Hill who had got his head opened up with a Gatorade bottle at a track meet, and I had gone with Charm to square off at some boys' houses who had been running their mouths too much.

And of course I had fought with everybody in my crew except Ricky, who was getting too much ass to fight, because if he won he could double destroy your ego. The best one to fight was Sawyer's brother Chester, who was always threatening you with a nut session or worse. I hoped that the beef would get squashed, but I thought that it would take a big-time older head to do it, and I thought he would have needed a .12 gauge or something with some heat. Because on that night, Woodlawn was coming thick.

We were just idling in the middle of the street, nigger shit, everybody talking at once, planning to fail, when the IROC-Z came up from behind, and the Monte Carlo and the EXP drove up from the other direction. The motherfuckers had some kind of CB or headphone communications. A crabapple-head big boy marched out of the Monte Carlo shouting, got up to my face and started yanking on the door handle. I know it: I had that pleading, begging look on my face. He swung on me anyway and then tried to rip me out from the AMC Sportabout, but the broken door handle saved me. My people, my people. Mighty Joe Young was riding shotgun, and he shouted at me, 'Drive!' I hit the gas and thread a needle through the IROC-Z–Cressida–EXP posse, racing my way down Chelsea Terrace. It was ride-or-die down the hill to Gwynns Falls Trail, Walbrook Junction, the briar patch for Charm, Pretty Ricky, and Knuckles.

Knowing the Junction better than our foes, we got

back to our block unscathed. I let out Ricky and his cousins, and then we cooled out in an alley. First the slickheads got Ricky's address from some girl and tried to raid his people's house, but they were in the middle of the block and Woodlawn couldn't get to a window or through the front door. I thought I had made a safe passage until the next morning my father woke me up and asked did anything happen. I told him no, and he walked me outside to the ride. Late that night, them damn County yos had chucked a wedge of concrete through the windshield of the wagon.

A couple of days later a homeboy who worked at the McDonald's on Liberty Heights, just over the line in the County, got banked. Charm and Knuckles stopped going up the 'Brook because Simon, the concrete thrower, had promised them a bullet. A week after that Pretty Ricky fought the cruelest of the host, Carlos Gallilee and Dante Rogers, in the middle of Reisterstown Road. For a cat known throughout the city as a gigolo, a guy with slanted eyes and a Puerto Rican look, Rick had a whole lot of heart. He knocked the knees out of his jeans beating those dogs off and he stayed with his cousins in Philadelphia for a couple of weeks after that.

The war went on at high schools, parties, football games, festivals, and public events. About two weeks after the chase, in the parking lot of the all-girls public senior high school where Muhammad, Dern, and I chilled out every day after track practice, this boy

Meechee was sitting in the back of a green Thunderbird steady loading a .38 while his homeboys, a lanky bastard about six foot nine and some other culprit, leaned on us. They cornered Muhammad on the hood of his Sentra.

'Where Ricky at? Where your boy at?'

I was wanting to run away with my whole body, but my feet got so heavy in the quicksand of his pistol that I could only look longingly in the direction of the administration building. My heart was pumping Cherry Coke the whole way but I was proud of Muhammad for how he kept the fear out of his voice. The next day Muhammad and Dern got their family arms and we went all tooled up to high school. They took it as far as slinging iron in their sport coats. The day after that, we cut school altogether for marksmanship class in Leakin Park, an abandoned grassland just west of the Junction that had become a desolate zone. The Pearls were jive giddy. I just blasted into the creek, but I had to stop Sawyer, who never had a whole lot of sense, from shooting the pistol right behind my ear. To my mind, nothing is as loud as the roar of that .38.

The war changed the landmarks of our scene. Up to that time I had been keen to play in the County, and I could have cared less about my grimy, down-on-its-heels hometown. Now that we had to go everywhere in groups for safety, Reisterstown Road Plaza Mall and Security Mall in the County, the places where we used to flock to scoop out the honey, were less inviting. Our neighborhood mall, Mondawmin, became safe – if we toned our flamboyance down a little – and we started falling through Mondawmin, the Harbor, even Old Town Mall on the East Side. We kept linking up with city cats we'd gone to school with or had been in summer programs with, guys I had known from church at Lafayette Square, or the Druid Hill Avenue YMCA, where my father had been the director. Plus the girls I knew from those parts of town were slinging enough iron to take care of a boy. We went to our cousins and neighbours from around our way to get our back, to hustlers I had worked with at minimum-wage jobs all over the city, who came from tiny-ass streets crammed with thousands of brick row houses. The kind of music a cat listened to, or how he cut his fade, became unimportant compared to if he was from the city, how good he was with his hands, and, especially, if he had heart. That was how Sonny got down with the clique, because even though he was a young boy, he had all of the above.

Heads from around my way cut their teeth on the Woodlawn beef. The hoppers, the young boys we never had room for in the car, they headed straight up to Bell and Garrison to build themselves up. The hustle on Garrison, or, even more big-time, Park Heights and Woodland, was strictly Fila and Russell. Man, them cats bumped. From then to now it must be something like three thousand cats shot on Garrison between the Junction and Pimlico – that's one boulevard in one section of one chocolate American city. Plus, ain't nobody ever see a bustling swaggering yipping corner like Park Heights and Woodland in its prime. Serving 'em well, boy and girl, serving 'em well. Knuckles and Mighty Joe Young knew how to get by around there. I never caught on and only went up to The Lot, the neighborhood McDonald's on Reisterstown Road, a couple of times. I wouldn't throw quarters away on Pac-Man or Space Invaders. I was spending my money on rugged-sole Timberlands and 12-inch records so I could become a club dancer. Same as slick, the corner was insular and monotonous, unless you had a taste for street fighting and raw booty. Anyway, the hoppers wound up getting tight with cats who the corner was all they had. Like Ringfrail's brother Clyde, who wore brass jewelry, or Taiwan, an adolescent beggar who graduated to being a teenage beggar. Or Little Toby, who had started smoking too early and would always be short and skinny. I think (and was glad) Wookie was already gone by then. I know, and was sad, that Monty was. Every time I go home and walk to the Korean store to get some Utz or Tastykake, I run into them all.

The young boys of course had to take it serious. I only had a year left of high school, but they were going to be in this thing for a long time. Pretty Ricky's younger brother Maceo started going to war on his own, against anybody at all. At the corner store on Wabash and Sequoia he stabbed Richard Franklin, who then followed Maceo back to his house and sent him three-quarters of the way to their family's funeral home with the same knife. Some vet's old bayonet. Kind of intimate, being punctured with the same steel that still has your victim's blood on it. When Five-O locked up Chucky Blue that same night, Chucky, on something like love boat, almost turned the paddy wagon over. That was pure dee Chuck Blue, living out the Myth. I'd never seen a motor vehicle rock from side to side on two wheels like that before.

It was curious. I found out a lot more about my neighborhood, and was surprised to know that I had a place in it. Slickheads from around the way, cats known for hanging on the corner, mad ill dynamite-style cats like Darius, who rode his Honda Elite scooter in Fila slippers – they respected preps from the city, as long as us cats carried that thing original, which was to say never perpetrated no fraud. It meant taking pride in where you're from. And we did. The Oxfords off Wabash were gaudy preps: pink shirts, green pants, bright-colored track shoes, and Gumby haircuts. Plus, there was no bourgeoisie contingent at the schools we mainly attended. Loyola, Walbrook, City College, Carver, Cardinal Gibbons, and Forest Park. To go to school there, you couldn't stand out more than to be an African American prep from the city. I might have eaten humble pie on a bus ride or two, but plenty of times I strutted the city like the word 'Hero' was stitched on my chest. And the best-known cat in the clique for that air of confidence was Sonny.

But then our style became a casualty in the war that went off and on for years. On account of the Woodlawn beef, everybody began to ease on down the road to slick, Russell sweats and Filas, bald head and sullen, gold in your mouth, pass the reefer. All of a sudden, it seemed like slick had something serene you needed to get through life, a good way to not mind being an outlaw. I didn't like it on a number of levels. And I was always the historian – the identity 'yo' was too much connected to the 'yo-ski' thing from the 1970s, when the kids ran 'What's up yoski?' into the fucking ground. And as I got more black and proud, the 'ski' part of it sounded too close to the Polack-Johnny level, the citywide hot dog stand. Corny for us to follow the hick klan from Dundalk and Highlandtown.

I never even knew all of exactly how we survived. I had a play cousin from Edmondson Village, slick as a wax floor and known throughout the city as The Ninja. He had jumped with the airborne in Grenada. One story went that he jogged up at a park on Woodlawn with an Uzi and told them to lay off. Another tale had it that the big-time boys from up the top of our street, who owned Yummy's at North and Gold, took an arsenal up to the courts at Bedford, where everybody from the County ran ball, and said they was holding so-and-so personally responsible for whatever went down. I admit, a couple of years later, one night we did have Carlos Gallilee all by himself up at Club 4604 on Liberty Heights. Darius, who had the distinction of having popped tool at the LL Cool J concert, wild Chuck Blue, and the ill James brothers were there, really wanting to hurt somebody. I just talked to Carlos, not feeling it was sporting to bring all of that wrath down on him on a night he was acting humble. But then again, he was an actor and today he's set himself up in Hollywood.

Funny how the slickheads didn't fare well in the end. Rocky, the mastermind – who had said up the Kappa House, not to me, just in my general direction, 'You and your homeboys is just fucked!' – shot in the head. Muscleman Dante, whose girl I stole, ended up strung-out after sitting down for ten at Jessup. Simon, the lunatic concrete-block man, gunned down at a police roadblock. I think pistol-loading Meechee fell into the dirt too – and, if he did, then that's too much like right.

Then again, now that I think of it, these were mainly city guys, who had hung strong with Woodlawn, 18 and 19 and, like me, trying anything to get out to the suburbs. Slickheads and their expensive tennis did win the style war; but, really, it was just that the city guys lost.

That summer, about ten weeks after the beef got underway, I learned that the police was the slave patrol and the Confederate Army extended. I had been surprised when they refused to protect me from the Woodlawn slickheads, but I hadn't known that my category was on their assassination list.

My father replaced the yellow wagon with a Japanese compact car, used, but with a tape deck and a sunroof, a real surprise. Somehow I had the car in the early afternoon, and me, Charm, and Mighty Joe Young were skylarking around the neighborhood, telling lies about the fine honey, bumping 'The Dominatrix Sleeps Tonight.' I noticed two white guys and a brother in a Chevrolet Cavalier near the library on Garrison, but I wasn't on the corner so it only seemed odd, not a personal threat. We stared them down and, three deep, drove off to the Plaza, doubling back and through, around Garrison Boulevard and Wabash Avenue.

At Reisterstown Road and Fords Lane I reached the traffic light. All of the sudden it seemed like a car was smashing into the side of me. A Highlandtown cracker pushed a heavy revolver through the sunroof and up to my head, his other hand reaching for the steering wheel. I could count the bullets in the chambers, and see the tiny indentations in the cones of the soft lead. I wet my lap. For real. I was preparing to die. The angry man was shouting, 'Move over!' and 'Git out the car! Git the fuck out the car!' Then, with some time, I thought to myself that he must be a damn bold car thief. It was broad daylight. And even though we had just bought the sporty little Toyota, I couldn't see why he'd be so amped up for a $7,890 car. In a minor key, I thought that a cool hustler would probably find some way to drive off.

I tried to throw the car in park and slide away from the gun at the same time, but I couldn't get past Charm Sawyer's legs in the passenger seat. Charm had been yoked halfway out of the window by the black gloved hand of . . . Five-O? I heard commotion in the back, and next thing I knew Mighty Joe Young had his teeth on the asphalt. Then I noticed a silvery patch swinging from the chest of the man from Highlandtown with the dirty beard, and he demanded my license and registration.

After about fifteen minutes the dirty white man came back to the car.

'You ran a red light back there but my buddy doesn't have enough time to write you a ticket. Beat it.'

I looked around fumbling with my mouth open and managed to get the Toyota away from the intersection. We got to the next block and pulled over, me and Charm shaking and crying from relief and shame and Mighty Joe Young mouthing Who-Struck-John. Never will get that dirty white man and that giant .38 from my mind.

When I told my father about it, I could see in his face and his demeanor that there was no authority to appeal to. When I was just a kid, I had been robbed by some bullies and had reluctantly confessed that humiliation to my dad. In his house shoes he stalked out into the middle of the avenue, attempting to find the boys who had wronged his child. But this new violation was just a new burden to shoulder. I knew enough to sense him crying on the inside. We were father and son inside of our house, but outside we were black males in America, with the same honor and respect as No. 1 crabs in season.

I guess Prep or Slick wasn't all that.

The Pell Grants and the Maryland scholarships got cut off around this time, and all of a sudden nobody was going to college out of state. The money went out as fast as the dope came in. That ride to Edwin Waters or Cheney or Widener, that had been wish fulfillment in the past. By the second half of the '80s, if you went to school, it was either down the street to the community college or up to Morgan, the old state college for Negroes where my parents and Charm's parents had been sent, at the end of the #33 bus line. Most of my homeboys, their parents would let them try it out for a semester. Our people believed in control. In our neighborhood fathers would brag to each other, 'I'm never letting that nigger drive my car,' meaning their own sons. Young boys like Dan Redd and Darryl and Mark were smart, but they couldn't get to school out of state and get that big jump on life from out the neighborhood. I got into college three hundred miles away – and those last weeks when the beef was running fast and furious, I tried not to be so simple-minded as to jeopardize a chance.

About two weeks before I was supposed to go off to Connecticut, a year now after the chase, the fellas wanted me to drive the brigade down to the Inner Harbor to square off against Woodlawn one last time. Remembering how my father's car had got kissed by the concrete block, I chilled. I heard that when it went down, it wasn't like a Murphy Homes versus Lexington Terrace scrap. Woodlawn had sent mainly the little boys. The police got into the fight before anybody got stomped, or thrown into the water. Still, everybody began their adult criminal record that night in '86, and later it helped me that I wasn't there. But I saved the car one night and burned it up the next. When I got back after my freshman year in college, still dropping off into sleep after six weeks on line for Kappa, I passed out at the wheel and hit a neighbor head-on. I never drove again until I was on my own.

They were dog years between the end of high school and the end of college. Time folded every summer: scrapping in '86, macking in '87, bent in '88, and banging a gun in '89. I wouldn't want to live through '89 again, bringing all of that time together. We weren't Oxfords so much anymore – just homeboys now – and only rocking the prep style as a kind of occasional comment on the absurdity of our condition. The world had turned Slick with a capital 'S.' To me the hi-top fade had its funeral rites when the cornball Toms at

Duke started wearing it. I even stopped collecting house music and let the Blastmaster speak for me with that record 'Ghetto Music.'

We knew what time it was, but used the powerful narcotics to keep ourselves from the numbers. Heroin was flowing like water that summer, and Saddlehead and Jidda, Paris and Los, all of them good ole North and Poplar Grove boys could get it. Poplar Grove. Longwood. Bloomingdale. The Junction. Then we started falling further down. In the wee hours we used to slumber outside some spot at Lombard and Arlington, not far from ole H. L. Mencken's, blunted, waiting for Troy and Stanley to finish sniffing that dope. The world of joogy. Around my way they call it 'boy' or 'joogy.' 'Girl' is 'Shirl' caine – after Shirley Avenue where you go get nice. If you live in a town with a lot of joogy, everything else, like girl, seems real regular, jive legal. Joogy got me down from the psychedelics that they pumped up at college. Put it like this: in a world of disarray, joogy helps you to carry that thing.

That summer, back from college, every time I left out the house I saw somebody with tool, and one time I'm making eye contact with this lean slickhead, shooting a .45 into the air to keep street fighters tearing up a park festival from scratching his Benz. When I caught his eye I thought he was going to finish me. No question, joogy helps keep that begging, crying look off of your face. It got to the point where the police would be detaining me for walking down the street, and I'm getting ill to handle the stress, which everybody say is imaginary. That summer of '89 people was cross and fussing and we used to wear our Africa medallions at these pro-black rallies organized by Public Enemy. The next summer, all the music was about killing each other over colored rags.

The summer Sonny got shot my right hand Charm Sawyer had to hit a boy who was holding a pistol on him, and even though I was making speed toward a degree, I doubted it was fast enough. Hanging out with Sawyer was scrapping every night, which wasn't really my style, especially after he busted my head on Muhammad's basement floor. Plus it's tough on your gear, my main way to get notice from the ladies. 'A yo, Lair, hold my glasses,' he'd say as he sized up someone for a scrap. 'Imma piece that nigger.' I would take them. Then he'd smirk and start throwing the dogs. He started out with skinny light-skin boys, but he was working his way up to short, wiry, dark-skin men. When we went out, he would always say that he would either get some pussy, beat a nigger, or get blind ill by the time the sun came up. I didn't understand his rage at the ceiling of possibility until a little later.

Charm got took over by the Myth, which had a couple of ingredients. The Myth meant crazy outrageous athleticism in every activity. It helped the style of it if the head of your thing went past your navel, but it all came together in an attitude of defiant obdurateness that we called Hard. I would try to cool him out, because I was being taught something different at school, but every time I wasn't around, he would trip the fuck out. At a party he shucked off all his gear and swung around ill until he got what he was looking for. One night Charm fouled a catatonic girl's mouth to stop niggers from running a train on her, but she still had to leave the city. He was getting known and some people were afraid of him. He had mastered the art of drilling any girl, no matter her look, no matter her size, at any time. Like, Pretty Ricky had written a book on the art of seduction. He had this snake-like way of peering into the eyes of the slinkiest, the trickiest, the flyest – the LaShawns, Letitias, Sheilas, and Keishas – the girls who had had so much exposure to slick that I didn't even know what to say to them. I only tried to win by light touch. But Charm didn't work in a whole lot of small talk or eye contact or hand-holding. He went on the Mandingo principle. He knocked down big China up against the freezer in my basement and she clawed grooves into his back. It took years for me to know what he did to make her cry out and lose control like that. She was so wide open every time we went with armloads of Guess apparel to the department store counter where she worked, it was like cashing a check.

I got a strong dose of the Myth too, the dream-world life of supernigger. One night of the dream me and Charm drank a couple of quarts of Mad Dog and picked up some wild ill broads from the Brook down at the Harbor. I only had one condom, used it on the girl I knew was out there, and ran raw in Sheba, thinking the odds were better because it was her time of the month. I thought another threshold of existence was at hand. Even the girls laughed about it, lil Lair happy cause he trimmed twice. The ill vibe kept clicking, though. At a party in the Junction Charm hit this boy in the face and broke his nose, and the jam was at the house of the broke-nose boy cousin. We had to fight Charm to get him out of there. Then, sitting five deep in a two-door Sentra trying to cool out, two hoppers came up on us. One skinny boy was on the street side, and a bald-headed light-skin boy with a shimmer in his mouth stood in the back. Skinny boy tapped the window with something metal. I heard a crack and the glass breaking, and we were all shouting to Pretty Ricky, 'Drive!' 'I'm hit!' I was pushing Charm and Knuckles so hard to peel away from that hot one searching for my ass. Decades of nightmares about that gunman.

About a week later, Sawyer and Sonny were throwing a cranker on Maryland Avenue, the little club district anchored by old-school Odell's (YOU'LL KNOW IF YOU BELONG, the T-shirt used to say), house music Cignel's, and citywide Godfrey's Famous Ballroom. All the young hustlers and fly girls hung out in that zone. I was a little late getting to the jam.

I'd get the feeling of supreme confidence and contentment, just walking up the street and wading into a real players' crowd. Hundreds deep with hustlers and fly girls – herb bumping – passing quarts of Mad Dog and Red Bull malt liquor. Knowing my hair was faded right and I was getting dap from the players and intimate touches from Sheila, Kim, Lisa, and Tanya. 'The Sound' by Reese and Santonio filling the air with our versions of the djembe, dundun, kenkeni, and sangban. Taking everybody way back. It's better than caine. Demerara. Ouagadougou.

Mighty Joe Young and me was nice, dipping up Murlin Avenue, near the bridge, gandering over to the zone from the Armory subway stop. All of a sudden, Ed from Bloomingdale drove by us and shouted, 'Sonny got shot!' Old school, we ran the mile or two down the street. Ten minutes later we're outside the operating room at University Shock Trauma, screaming on the state trooper and the young Asian lady doctor who said, 'Your friend didn't make it.' She spat out that shit to me like I put the gun on Sonny.

I felt like the hospital was run by people with the slickhead mentality, that mentality that claims a nigger ain't shit. Me, I always wanted to redeem a nigger. The state trooper, a brother who understood, saved that bitch's Chinese ass. I wanted to do something. Sonny's parents came in a few minutes later. Crushed. Crying scene. Me and Mighty Joe Young walked down to the central police station where they were taking Sawyer's statement. We were amped up, spreading the word at hangouts like Crazy John's and El Dorado's, where we ran into some of our people.

Sawyer had been standing next to Sonny when they got stuck up. Sawyer's antsy brother Chester had a few dollars on him and gated up the alley, so Sawyer and Sonny, on the other side of the car, booked for it too. Rodney, Birdman, Dern, and Rock could only stand with their hands in the air while the runners gave it up. Sonny and a guy sitting on some steps got shot by a .22 rifle.

A lot of people blamed Sawyer for Sonny's murder, but I told him I was happy he had made it. He was my boy. We had been lightweight wilding up until then. No QP, no Z, no eight ball, no stick-up, no home invasion, no pop-tool, no cold-blooded train. Sawyer, James Brown, and Rock had taken a white boy for bad once. And Sawyer had been seen running down the street with a television, which had kind of got the police looking. Omar had taken a girl's telephone and her father's horse pistol. Sawyer and I had run a couple of gees on some wild young girls, and one time a grown woman did start fussing, but it was his cousin. I remember, because I left my high school graduation watch at her house. I thought if you were going to do the do, you had to take off everything.

One night a little boy who had connections had tried to kill James Brown with a bat down at Cignel's, and we beefed over our heads, but James Brown let the thing go. I don't know how many times I got in a car with folk I ain't really know, on their way from or to do I don't know what. It was all right there. Rock, Darius,

Worly, Chucky, Taft, Fats, Paris, Wood, Flip, Yippy, Champ, Ringfrail, Hondo, Reds. A whole lot of people got caught up in the mix.

What really hurt everybody was that Sonny had a whole lot of heart. He was a stand-up cat who had the will to make a difference. Shirt-off-his-back type of cat. Break a bottle over a big nigger's head for you cat. If the police looked for the killers, three men and a woman, they never found anybody. I had been in the Five-O palace on Baltimore Street and seen them lounging like they were on the whites-only floors. I had seen an office with a Confederate flag in it and some other of that old-timey, Frederick County shit. They always acted like Sonny's murder was 'drug-related,' like half of three hundred other murders that year. It hurts to think about his unsolved killing, twenty years later.

After Sonny's funeral, we started linking with cats who had hurt people, hoping to luck up onto that stick-up boy with the letter G on his hat who had gunned him down. The night after they shot Sonny we ganged into a dark room lit by the dutchy going around. A powerfully muscled old head addressed the mourning circle. 'I gits a nut every time I pull the trigger.' None of us ever forgot his sincerity. He said it to us like he was confessing something deep and personal, something that came out of the soul. I believed him.

Since Sonny had finished a year at Morehouse, the less stand-up guys figured that life wasn't worth struggling for. They started to get ill after the funeral like it was a paying job. I knew I didn't have as much heart as Sonny, so I did my share in the dim rooms. The morning after the funeral me and Clifton tried to run a gee on a young girl with a glass eye, not knowing she was five seconds from tricking on the corner – and Clifton months away hisself from the cemetery. Sometimes you would even pity a cat and bip half that bag of dope so that they wouldn't get hooked. One reason I stopped getting high was that Rock, my man from the bus stop days, pulled me up strong about looking weak, chasing. Sometimes you need to see yourself through the eyes of someone who has looked up to you. Then he got caught with a package and sat down at the department of corrections at Jessup, so I really tried to pull my pants up. After about eighteen months, overdoses began and cats started heading out of state to get away. Then there were the guys among us who thought that joogy wouldn't get to them, since they weren't shooting it up. But next thing, they started flashing pistols to the countergirl at Roy Rogers. That gets you a seven-year bit at Hagerstown, or you could get lucky and go to Jessup where people at least can visit you.

A couple of the cats really tried to make a fortune. If Sawyer was my right hand, then Muhammad was my heart. When I decided to make a break for school in 1990, after my father went back to Guinea, Muhammad told me soberly, 'Lair. Imma make a million dollars this year.' The hustler thing was in the air. All of the rap music was trying to help you know the I Ching of Rayful and Alpo and our hometown man Peanut King. We all knew by heart the DC anthem 'Stone Cold Hustler' and G Rap's 'Road to the Riches.' But I was so deep into reading about the COINTELPRO thing and what they did to Dr. Martin Luther King Jr. that none of the stories about stacking chips could reach me. Besides the fact that all the New York cats at school would be flipping out over the Bodymore stories I was telling, or the time my homeboys fell through for a visit, joogy-deep. Anyway, Muhammad acted hurt when I looked away from him.

For about two years, we didn't have that much rap for each other, a homeboy blood problem. Meanwhile, Muhammad tried to get water from the rock with Rodney Glide. They stretched out until they tripped. Eventually, the state of Pennsylvania took the wind out of Glide's sails for eight years, twenty-nine miles west of Philly at Graterford. I remember reading the newspapers about the old crew when I was in graduate school in California, a million miles away.

Sawyer turned the Myth in a new direction. He laid up with a Jamaican sister, got back in school, and earned a degree. He won an internship with a congressman from the streets who knew where he was coming from. He started working with the hoppers at George B. Murphy Homes high-rises, before it got blown up to make way for condos and the university hospital, where they work on getting the bug out. Just going down to Murphy Homes was a trip to us back in the day, where life and death, crime and punishment was wide open, like at my cousin's house on Myrtle Avenue, where Carmello's from. 'Fat Boy's out! Fat Boy's out! Girl on green. Girl on green,' is how the touts would run it down.

Sonny dying like he did definitely motivated me to finish graduate school and teach at the university level. But going to college for eleven years was, no doubt, the most sterile experience I had known. It was feeling all balled up like an English walnut. An experience that seemed designed to make me question who I was, if I was a man or not, if I was doing something worthwhile or not. On top of it all, it trained you to appreciate everything about old master and them, right down to studying their trifling distinctions, which is why I guess not that many brothers, when they know this thing about the war, bother with school.

After some years in the trenches, Sawyer got hooked up by George Soros. Now he has a company trying to help 'at risk' young people. I guess he helped himself. Sawyer stood for one thing, and I got down with him on it. 'Just put it out there. No matter who it hurts, whether it's a lie or not, right or wrong, good or bad. Never stop putting it out there.'

[2012]

Christopher Glazek

– Hasids vs. Hipsters –

The figure of the woman assumes its most seductive aspect as a cyclist. . . . In the clothing of cyclists the sporting expression still wrestles with the inherited pattern of elegance, and the fruit of this struggle is the grim sadistic touch which made this ideal image of elegance so incomparably provocative to the male world.
– Walter Benjamin, *The Arcades Project*

This is our shtetl, and our walls must go high.
– Grand Rebbe Zalmen Teitelbaum, Satmar Hasidic leader

Near the end of *Who Framed Roger Rabbit*, after Roger, Jessica, and Eddie are captured by weasels and delivered to the Acme factory, Judge Doom, the film's malefactor, reveals his plan to exterminate the inhabitants of Toontown. His objective, expressed in contemporary terms, is nation-building. And his means of ethnic cleansing? 'Several months ago,' Doom declares, 'I had the good providence to stumble upon this plan of the City Council's. A construction plan of epic proportions! They're calling it a *freeway*.' In 1988, when the film came out, public works had lost their power to awe, but Doom, speaking in a fictionalized

1947, was right to get caught up in reverie. Toontown would be rubble, its infrastructure swapped for 'eight lanes of shimmering cement running from here to Pasadena.'

The Bloomberg administration's 2008 commitment to build a 14-mile *greenway* connecting Bay Ridge and Greenpoint in Brooklyn – roughly the distance between Pasadena and West Hollywood – differed from Judge Doom's plan in some particulars. Instead of the gas stations, motels, fast-food hubs, and 'wonderful, wonderful billboards!' that Doom giddily anticipates, the Mayor's cycling agenda envisaged an urban arcadia punctuated by sleek commutes, elfin waistlines, and extravagant landscaping. Just as in Paris, where a fashion-forward bike-lending program enlivened the presidential prospects of the sprightly Bertrand Delanoë, so, in New York, would the dwarfish Michael Bloomberg ride the two-wheeled wonder to the summits of environmental stardom.

By the summer of 2009, Bloomberg's transport chief, Janette Sadik-Khan, was already crowing, somewhat implausibly, that New York City had become 'the bicycling capital of the United States.' If the administration's ecotopian hard-liners got their way, the city would soon boast a cycling culture to rival even the extremist enclaves of northern Europe – Amsterdam, Berlin, Copenhagen – where cowed locals live in terror of importuning bike bells, the streets hostage to biker autocracy.

But first Bloomberg had to win reelection. In the months before the vote, Chinatown residents started complaining about a bike lane installed on Grand Street, asserting that speeding bicyclists posed a danger to ambulating oldsters. Truckers in Staten Island responded even more furiously, clinging to their vanishing parking spaces and chasing down any bikers who got in their way. The most intractable objections came from South Williamsburg, where the Satmars, a sect of Hasidic Jews, complained that a freshly consecrated bike lane on Bedford Avenue drew in a bad element: irresponsibles who flouted traffic laws and imperiled the neighborhood's many schoolchildren, who had to ford a river of cyclists when descending from the district's Hebrew-lettered school buses. The Yiddish-speaking Satmars referred to these unruly passers-through as '*Artisten*.' The rest of the city called them hipsters.

Hipsters had their own ideas about what was rankling the Satmars. As early as 2003, Williamsburg's Hasidic population had protested against a wave of so-called 'yuppies,' Manhattan transplants who brought high rents and loose morals. At a community board meeting, Hasidic participants denounced an expensive development on Broadway, in the shadow of the Williamsburg Bridge, as 'an extension of the East Village,' and a 21-year-old Hasidic attendee warned of 'a very liberal lifestyle.' 'We have Jewish housing, synagogues, a Jewish medical center,' he pointed out. The newcomers favored 'bars and swimming pools. We don't like these things.' A rabbi cast doubt on the new residents' 'morality,' deeming them 'dangerous to our children.'

Four years later, as land prices crept upward amid upper-middle-class youth migration, bike lanes came to South Williamsburg. At another board meeting on September 8, 2008, Hasids called on the city to remove new bike lanes on Wythe and Bedford Avenues and to postpone construction on a planned lane for Kent Avenue. Although the Hasid opposition presented several rationales for opposing the lanes, including, once again, the safety of children exiting school buses and the loss of parking spaces, the most explosive motive was articulated by board member Simon Weisser, who told the *New York Post* that he was perturbed by clothing. 'I have to admit, it's a major issue, women passing through here in that dress code,' he said. 'It bothers me, and it bothers a lot of people.' To hipsters, this showed the Satmars' true colors – they were oppressors! That very summer, the Satmars had complained about a billboard visible from the Brooklyn-Queens Expressway featuring the swim-suited cast of 90210. Earlier in the decade, the community had been similarly aggrieved by a billboard for *Sex and the City*. The Satmars weren't worried about safety, they were worried about erotic danger. And if the Satmars wanted to make this about sex, then sex was what they'd get!

The city's Department of Transportation, observing events from its headquarters on Worth Street in lower Manhattan, suddenly found itself cast in the role of a colonial viceroy forced to adjudicate between warring indigenous tribes. Of course, neither of the Williamsburg disputants could be classed 'indigenous' in any rigorous sense – the Satmars began to arrive in the late 1940s, the hipsters in the late 1990s; and, really, tribes at least usually share some common history, some deeper connection to a region. Maybe the hipsters and the Hasids started to seem more like cartoons.

A friend of mine, raised in a Reform Jewish household, likes to joke that the most transgressive thing she could do would not be to marry another woman, or get addicted to heroin, but to become a Hasid. Satmars don't proselytize, but Lubavitchers famously do, and one of the reasons America's Hasidic population has grown so dramatically in recent decades is that they've found converts among once-secular Jewish youth.

There's a logic to this. At their most extreme, hipsters and Hasids present rival heresies, dueling rejections of bourgeois modernity. That each group selected Williamsburg as the terrain for carving out a secessionist utopia can only be blamed on the cunning of history, plus the L train.

The symmetry is powerful, if accidental. Both factions are marked by recognizable hairstyles and unusual modes of dress. Where the hipster wardrobe is ever-changing – one day it's trucker hats, overalls, and chin straps, the next it's fedoras, onesies, and bangs – the Satmar uniform has proven stable over 70 years: white shirts, pants, three-piece suits, shtreimel fur hats, and *payes* side braids for the men; shin-length dresses and sumptuous wigs for the women. Both groups are resented by their near relations (ordinary bourgeois youth, mainstream Jews) for their economic dependence on others – hipsters on their parents and/or arts and non-profit funding, and Hasidim on charity: despite pockets of wealth, one third of Hasidic families in Williamsburg receive some form of public assistance.

Both groups live in configurations unusual for the advanced capitalist west. Hipsters often live with multiple roommates, encouraging a wide variety of romantic, or worryingly platonic, entanglements. Hasids live in enormous families. The *average* size of a Satmar family is nine people. It would not be unusual to enter either a hipster or a Satmar apartment and see a cot in the kitchen.

For all its medieval costuming, Satmar Hasidism is a relatively recent phenomenon. The various Hasidic splinter groups – Lubavitcher, Satmar, Belz – trace their roots to the mid-18th century, when the mystic rabbi Israel Ba'al Shem Tov gained a following for his anti-scholastic, kabbalistic revision of Orthodox Judaism. The Satmars, a large and particularly conscientious division of Hasidim, were founded only in the 20th century, by Grand Rebbe Joel Teitelbaum, who would have been murdered by the Nazis had his freedom not been purchased from Adolf Eichmann by the Zionist Rudolph Kastner. Nevertheless, Teitelbaum hated the Zionists, even blaming them for the Holocaust.

Teitelbaum arrived in New York with a small retinue on Rosh Hashanah in 1946 (5707, on the Jewish calendar), where he founded a synagogue and set for himself the task of recreating the cloistered world of Satu Mare, the Hungarian shtetl whence the Satmars sprang. Fur hats, Talmud study, and procreation were the order of the day. From an original colony with a reputed population of only ten after World War II, the Satmar population in Brooklyn, bolstered by immigration, grew by 2006 to more than 35,000. Although parts of the community are plagued by poverty, the Williamsburg Satmars are better off than the co-religionists in the upstate refuge of Kiryas Joel, which is often called the poorest place in the United States. The downstaters got into Brooklyn real estate before several rounds of booms, and they also entered the traditional diamond business.

The Satmars speak Yiddish to each other. Their major paper, *Der Yid*, has a circulation of 50,000, roughly on par with the *London Review of Books* (about half as many as *Vice Deutschland*). Hipsters, too, have long evinced an affection for Yiddish, especially when combined with accordions, as in Klezmer music. Franz

Kafka, a significant hipster if not the original one, had a weakness for Yiddish theater.

Like other schismatic spin-offs, Satmars and hipsters have struggled to maintain unity in the face of generational succession. As Michael Powell reported for *New York*, the death of charismatic founder Rebbe Joel in 1981 left the Satmars looking to his nephew, Moses Teitelbaum, to take the top spot. Although Moses never matched Joel's appeal, the community continued to grow and prosper. Moses' eldest son, Aaron Teitelbaum, seemed the heir apparent, but in his last months of life Moses decided to annoint his third son instead, Zalmen. Aaron cried foul, triggering repeated convocations of the Beis Din, the Satmar religious court. In 2006, the New York State Court of Appeals refused to help resolve the matter, calling the internal religious dispute 'non-justiceable.' Though less litigious, hipsters in Williamsburg have also been riven by inter-cohort tensions, as the aging early pioneers have added baby boutiques to Bedford Avenue, attracting the derision of younger migrants.

Amid these fears of community dissolution, rumors of bike lane confrontation began to swirl on both sides. Hipsters, for their part, started to resent the increasingly bellicose tone of epithets hurled at them on Bedford Avenue by angry, black-hatted pedestrians. Although the insults were delivered in Yiddish – Yiddish commanding much hipster enthusiasm but little comprehension – the cyclists got the drift. One familiar tale repeated in online cycling forums warned of a club-wielding bus driver who would chase and threaten to maim any hipster who complained about his parking job. Was the neighborhood lurching toward an anti-hipster pogrom?

One particularly terrifying legend featured a character referred to as the Ginger Hasid rapist. This tale, a bizarre hipster refraction of the Hasids' anxiety about over-sexed 'artists,' turned predator into prey. In the story, a fresh-faced hipster ganymede returns to his rented room late at night and finds an obese, red-haired Orthodox visitor hiding in the closet. On discovery, the Hasid rapist attempts to kiss the boy, running away at the first show of resistance. That this shadowy figure was essentially non-violent, boy-friendly, and not actually a rapist at all, did nothing to reduce his fascination.

In the fall of 2009, Bloomberg squeaked into a third term with just over fifty percent of the vote. Four weeks later, the city announced its decision to remove fourteen blocks of bike lane from Bedford Avenue between Flushing and Division. Seth Solomonow, a spokesman for the Department of Transportation, described the move as 'part of ongoing bike network adjustments in the area.' Others described it as a quid-pro-quo, the fruit of a deal struck with Satmar leaders on the eve of the election. Solomonow encouraged bikers to use a new two-way lane on Kent Avenue and a barrier-protected connector lane on Williamsburg Street. A spokesman from the Mayor's office called the replacement route 'the Cadillac of bike paths.'

Initial hipster reaction was angry but peaceful. A group dressed as clowns led a funeral procession along Bedford to protest the decision, but failed to capture the public imagination since they lacked any vernacular of protest other than the language of a grant application. 'Enforced, protected bike lanes save cyclist lives, improve the landscape and make better use of public space for most of the community,' said the clowns.

Others tried action: they would repaint the bike path. The first repainting attempt took place in two sessions, one on Friday, November 27th – the Sabbath – and the second on Sunday, November 29th. The painters posted a video on YouTube documenting their rolling, spraying, and stenciling exploits. The video mimics the DIY-charm of Trading Spaces. Its hipster protagonists look handy and youthful. The sequence ends with a service announcement printed in four installments in stark white letters. 'We are New York City bicyclists, and our message is clear: Don't take away our bike lanes./ We use this stretch of Bedford Avenue because it is a direct route to the Williamsburg Bridge./ We will continue to use it whether or not there is a bike lane there, but not having one puts us at greater risk from cars./ That's why bike lanes exist – for safety. Do not try to remove them, or we will put them back for our own safety.'

Here the hipsters employed the unmistakable register of a teenager trying to 'use reason' with adults. The strategy is to appeal first to safety concerns, then to the inevitability of transgression in the event of a ruling against the child.

Repainting was nearly complete when the hipsters met the Satmars' neighborhood vigilante unit, the Shomrim, who 'bear-hugged' the vandals until the NYPD arrived. Although the police made no arrests that night, after the video posting and Satmar complaints, repainters Quinn Hechtropf and Katherine Piccoci were eventually arrested for 'criminal mischief' and 'defacing the street.' Hechtropf, defiant in defeat, proclaimed himself a 'self-hating Jewish hipster.'

Escalating the conflict after the apprehension of Hechtropf and Piccoci, hipsters planned a naked bike ride along the old funeral route. Calling themselves 'freedom riders,' a group organized by Heather Loop, a 27-year-old bike messenger, arranged to meet at the Wreck Room, a Flushing avenue hipster redoubt, and ride together to the Williamsburg Bridge in underwear, breasts exposed. 'If you can't handle scantily clad women,' Loop told reporters, you should 'live in a place where you can have your own sanctuary, like upstate.' But Loop had the misfortune of selecting one of the coldest days of the winter. Attendance was low, and no one rode naked, though some riders pinned fake rubber breasts over their wool coats.

Hipsters then invited the Hasidic community to engage in a public debate. On January 25th, 2010, an open discussion was held at Pete's Candy Store on Lorimer St. – hardly neutral territory, which may have accounted for the fact that only three Satmars showed up, the activist Isaac Abraham and two adjuncts. As Michael Idov reported in an article for *New York*, Abraham held his own in an overwhelmingly biker-friendly crowd, speaking with conviction against disrespectful speed-demons (he revealed in the course of the evening that his wife had been the victim of a biker hit-and-run). The hipsters parried with their own horror stories, including the one about a bus driver with a club. At one point, an exasperated Abraham asked, 'So in other words, what you're saying is I should go back to the community and say that I just got a message, it's their way or the highway?' To which the officially impartial moderator responded, 'Their way IS the highway!'

After the event, a blogger on FreeWilliamsburg.com conceded that Abraham had seemed genuinely concerned about the safety of pedestrians, paving the way for a return to hipster placidity. During the debate Caroline Samponaro, an activist with Transportation Alternatives, had pointed out that bikers and pedestrians were both 'awesome,' and 'should be working together, not against each other.' Her solution, or her attempt at one, was to call for the establishment of 'Waving Wednesdays,' during which she would ride with a group of hipsters at rush hour through the zone of contention and wave at Hasidic pedestrians to 'improve safety and morale' and foster a 'positive, communal atmosphere.'

The Doña Marina figure in this drama, who spoke not only to the demands of hipster and Hasid, but also, and most emphatically, to the demands of the press, is Baruch Herzfeld, a 38-year-old lapsed Satmar who runs a used bike shop called Traif Bike Gesheft – 'the unkosher bike shop.' Herzfed moderated the Pete's Candy Store debate, a position won on the strength of his reputation as a go-between. His Gesheft offered bikes to Satmar patrons at reduced prices. But Herzfeld sided with the hipsters during the bike lane controversy. He has been referred to as the 'unofficial spokesman' of the repainters, although the extent of his involvement is unclear.

A couple blocks from Herzfeld's 'Gesheft' is a pork-anchored restaurant also called 'Traif' that caters to both hipsters and to Hasids on the down low. Predictably, real hipsters prefer Gottlieb's, the kosher Hasidic deli around the corner. In a *Wall Street Journal* article examining hipster/Hasid commercial exchange, a 25-year-old motorcycle-racing trust funder explained that Gottlieb's has 'everything – good food, good prices, irony.'

Up and down Lee Avenue, the Satmar SoHo, men charge along in pairs and children scurry, stopping occasionally to tug at their beleaguered mothers. Scattered through the neighborhood are well-trafficked playgrounds. There, little Satmars, boys and girls, run, play, scream and *ride* – wheeling around with impunity on a wide range of scooters, wagons, bikes, and tricycles: the mayor's cavalry-in-training.

Evidence of a thaw mounted throughout the spring. In May, the Sundance hit *Holy Rollers* premiered in New York, starring a side-curled Jesse Eisenberg as a young Hasid from Williamsburg who winds up working as an ecstasy mule in the transatlantic drug trade. Hipsters noted that Eisenberg's role was difficult to distinguish from the Jewish adolescent he played in Noah Baumbach's *Squid and the Whale*.

On June 27, 2010, the MTA enacted a package of alterations to New York subway routes with uncertain implications for the neighborhood depicted in Eisenberg's Hasid debut. The once-sleepy M train, which had been widely rumored to be slated for elimination, instead emerged a winner, annexing the V line and with it a direct route from South Williamsburg through SoHo, the West Village, and Midtown. The now-vanished Bedford bike lane had been used by hundreds of people every day. The M train is used by a hundred thousand.

Historically, a certain caliber of hipster always preferred South Williamsburg to its modish northern cousin, anyway – much as a certain caliber of Manhattanite has only ever been to South Williamsburg to dine at Peter Luger, the century-old steak house. Now Williamsburg's South-siders – hipster purists and Satmar worshippers accustomed to seclusion – will find themselves in one of the newly most convenient and underpriced neighborhoods in the one of the biggest and most covetous cities in the world. They should enjoy it while it lasts.

[2011]

Kristin Dombek

– How to Quit –

We do not know how to renounce anything, Freud once observed. This type of relation to the object indicates an inability to mourn. The addict is a nonrenouncer par excellence.
– Avital Ronell, *Crack Wars*

The way of life is wonderful; it is by abandonment.
– Ralph Waldo Emerson, 'Circles'

Two blocks east of the river, beside the Williamsburg Bridge, stands a white factory building, seven stories tall, whose windows look onto the bridge and across the river to Manhattan and over the neighborhood's low rooftops and famous water towers. It is 2011, but this building hasn't yet been cubed up into condos. Inside, it still looks like 1994, each floor a maze of ad hoc lofts, studios, galleries, and workshops, the stained hallways thick with strange smells and years of dust.

A couple of years ago during a party a kid from some band jammed the freight elevator between floors, tried to jump out, fell, and died; the elevator still isn't working. So to get into the building, you climb steep factory flights of gray stairs up away from the basement, where a giant machine rumbles. By the fifth or sixth floor, it is hard to breathe. It is winter, and the rumbling is a steam heater. Every few hours, it blows scalding-hot, wet air up through clanking pipes into the lofts. All over the building tenants open windows, and long white curtains flutter in the hissing steam. Outside, people are climbing up the steep slope of the bridge's pedestrian walkway, on foot or skateboard or bicycle. Only a few look at the building, and even fewer try to glimpse inside. I am in here, watching the bridge and chain-smoking.

The sun sinks down behind the bridge, filling this big white room with warm red light. When a J, M, or Z train passes, the room darkens and then flushes red again. The sky turns red, then orange, then indigo, then starless, like every Brooklyn night. It's happy hour. Half the neighborhood is already drunk on two-for-one drafts or shot-and-PBR deals. All week, the kids in lofts and storefronts who do under-the-radar marketing for creative agencies in other lofts and storefronts have been chasing Oxy with Adderall and Adderall with Oxy. Now they're pulling bottles of tequila from their desk drawers and texting their dealers. A country band is carrying banjos into the Rod and Gun Club. They're sound-checking at Trash Bar and lighting the fire at Union Pool. The Shabbos siren sounds across the south side. It's almost time to go out.

Snow came on Halloween weekend this year, fat slow flakes falling on the bridge, turning the scene outside the windows all industrial Courier and Ives, the Gretsch Building just a wide gray ghost beyond the trains. There was a cold wind blowing the slush around, and I watched people breaking their umbrellas against it and struggling to walk, sliding carefully on the sidewalk. This was the day the heat turned on. First, a clanking from below and up through the walls, then the sound of rushing water, and then, in the large sculptor's studio that I've turned into my writing room, a sound like a teapot ready to blow. Steam shot upward from the end of one of the pipes, and water poured and pooled on the floor. I braced for an explosion but it turns out this happens every time the building warms up. It only sounds catastrophic.

That afternoon a guitar player on a dead-mother bender was walking over from Bushwick in the snow to fuck me, his feet wrapped in plastic bags inside his Converse because he's too broke to buy boots. I walked down six flights to let him in. I hadn't seen him sober before, which was why I'd requested the afternoon appointment, but I'd stashed a fresh liter of Jack Daniels above the fridge. The lighting in the stairway was pulsing and dim. Snow from the roof was melting down the yellowed walls and pooling on the landings. We didn't kiss in the entryway. We made small talk as we wound our way up around the puddles, through the industrial waterfall. A few minutes later I was on my knees. The next week I bought new boots myself – short black boots that lace up, boots from the time of coal and steam, but with heels so high they are always sexual.

I am in this building but I am thinking of another white factory building, ten blocks behind me, beside the river. In 1999 I was living with a friend in a railroad apartment on North 7th by the Brooklyn–Queens Expressway that smelled of cheap floor varnish and mildew, no matter what we did. After we moved in, the upstairs neighbors told us that the landlord had kicked out a Puerto Rican family with four children and doubled the rent to $1,200, which was almost too much for us. Then a bike messenger we knew heard some friends of his were building lofts in an old textile warehouse on North 3rd. We walked to the river and up five flights of stairs, into a massive room with a wall of windows looking out onto the river and the whole bright city, a place as thrilling as a cathedral, as beautiful and sad as the person you fall in love with when you already know he will break your heart. We knew we'd be kicked out and priced out, just as we'd kicked out and priced out the Puerto Ricans. But we had to get into this building anyway, and to afford it we had to get our deposit back.

This was our plan: the bike messenger would ride by our apartment and throw a brick through the window wrapped in a note that read, Yuppies go home. I'd call the cops, file a police report, and then call our landlord crying, saying the neighborhood was unsafe and could we get our deposit back. But the day before we were to execute this ingenious conspiracy, my boyfriend at the time, a sweet-eyed punk kid from New Orleans who was a drug dealer and had some experience with the police, convinced me that I'd never make it through the report because of what a bad liar I am, according to him. So we gave up, lost our deposit, borrowed money from the bike messenger (who somehow always had more than we did), and moved in.

My share of the rent was $650. I cannot hope to capture for you the happiness of sitting by those windows and watching slow barges guided down the river by bright red tugboats, the buildings of Manhattan transformed every hour by different sunlight, and the mesmerizing plows of the waste transfer station next door, pushing around piles of garbage among beautiful brightly colored dumpsters. There were five years of potlucks and parties, bands and shows, cross-genre multimedia interactive technology performative collaborative art projects. The towers collapsing across the river, military tanks rolling down Bedford Avenue, then all the war protests. A man to fall in love with, a beautiful ex-junkie and sometime pain-reliever addict who moved in next door. All our nights spent in bars, the fucking in bathrooms, the lines snorted in back booths after close, the shouting on sidewalks, fucking all the way up those five flights of stairs as the sun came up. You have been young, or you are young, and you know that story, and you know the story of this neighborhood, or you think you do. The landlords began trying to force us out so they could build multimillion-dollar condos, and I moved east with the ex-junkie, as everyone was having to do, east to the Williamsburg of the Italians, in our case. My rent tripled, and soon the world felt like it was ending. I started dreaming of a quiet garden apartment in Boerum Hill or Prospect Heights, away from 22-year-olds and condo buildings. But when I left him, I moved back here, to the old but now unrecognizable neighborhood, into this building that looks like the building where I met him, or how it used to look.

Beyond the bridge, the Gretsch Building lights up. Inside it rich people are having cocktail hour, or something. I can't see them. The Gretsch was a musical instrument factory, then full of artists. In 1999, the management company began to turn the water and electricity and heat off, then on again, then off. In this way, they drove the tenants out. Now it has a granite lobby, glass elevators, a meditative waterfall, and units with Sub-Zeros and exposed concrete beams and floating fireplaces framed in Pietra Colombino limestone. Some people think Beyoncé lives in there. I haven't seen her, but I've seen the rest of it, thanks to the dullest New Year's Eve party ever. Starting in the late '90s, dozens more loft buildings pushed out their live/work tenants. Our old textile warehouse was one of the latest, in 2006. After the eviction, architects carved out an atrium and built a lobby out of *2001: A Space Odyssey* – glossy white and grand, flanked by strange asymmetrical hallways. They leveled the waste transfer station and built The Edge and then Northside Piers, thirty-some stories each of tacky glassy condos, and in their basements were pools, 'golf systems,' screening rooms. These buildings gave you the feeling that when the apocalypse came to Williamsburg, they'd float up into space in luminous self-sufficiency and orbit the wrecked planet while their residents gathered in the billiards room, drank complex cocktails, and eyed each other's neoprene skinny jeans.

But gentrification is the opposite of the apocalypse. The apocalypse would pause history, level the built world to a pile of trash, and most likely lower rents considerably. Gentrification churns history forward, takes out the trash, carts away rubble, hides the poor, makes you work more and more to manage your rent, and encrypts the past, when you didn't have to work so many jobs just to fucking live here, behind its glossy surfaces. To distract us from this decimation of the past and the poor it opens restaurants and bars that simulate other pasts. The old beer and liquor outlet on the corner of North 3rd and Berry, where we used to rent kegs for parties, is now an old-time German beer garden, its waitresses' breasts plumped cartoonishly by little German beer garden corsets. Across the street, where Slick's motorcycle repair shop was for years, there's a gleaming skate and surf store. There are half a dozen speakeasy-type cocktail bars with handlebar-mustached bartenders. There are three diners quaint enough to make your heart ache. There's Marlow & Sons and the rest of the country-living places, where you eat surrounded by animal trophies and decorative farm tools. There are old-time ice cream shops, general stores, old-time down-home barbecue joints, old-time down-home fried chicken joints, and rustic ski lodge–style restaurants. There is every past you could ever imagine, but little you remember.

When a neighborhood changes this much this fast it feels like either the old neighborhood was the real one and this one is some kind of monstrous double, or if this neighborhood is real, then that old one must always have been a lie.

If the old neighborhood was real, this building is a steam-powered time machine. If the new neighborhood is real, this building is a dream, or a crypt.

In other words, all this building makes me want to do is drink and fuck. I'm in here, sipping whiskey to blunt some postcocaine jitters, and rolling Bali Shag cigarettes to save money.

The music of this winter is the soundtrack to the movie *Drive*. Everyone in the neighborhood is talking about it. The bartender across the street plays it every time he works. I see the movie by myself one afternoon at the

Nitehawk on Metropolitan, where the sound is good and you can get food. I order a Bloody Mary, carefully, not sure how my voice sounds or if my face looks right, because I've been fucking the guitar player for the past twenty-four hours. We're on MDMA, which has turned us into a science experiment. We get within a foot of each other and we have to fuck again. He goes down on me indefinitely.

At first it's normal, and then he drops down into some deep, quiet place of absolute and perfect concentration. He is patient, he waits, barely moving, but he turns us from two people into liquid, and I come and come. Finally we stop because he has to go to band practice, and so I go see this movie. In the theater my legs are weak and I keep checking to make sure I'm fully clothed and my face is burning and everyone seems to be looking at me curiously. The ecstasy is tingling out gently; it's not going to be one of those suicidal E hangovers; everything is luscious and precise. When the music starts, I can feel it in the seat. Soft, thumping bass beats, pulsing in and out in waves, sometimes with sweet synthesized little-girl voices singing on top of them. College and Electric Youth's 'A Real Hero': 'You have proven to be/ A real human being and a real hero.' Desire's 'Under Your Spell': 'I don't eat/ I don't sleep/ I do nothing but think of you.'

The driving is perfect. Ryan Gosling's silent maneuvers, his watching, his listening. The first driving scene is remarkable for its pauses – the way he waits, the way he doesn't drive, hiding the car under an overpass, parking on a side street while the cops drive by. He says nearly nothing and he moves only as much as he absolutely has to. He barely speaks to Carey Mulligan, who has the face of a very young girl. But he takes her on a drive and smiles at her and helps her with her groceries and her car and her son and presumably they fall in love. Their scenes pulse with nothing being said, the way the scenes in *Twilight* pulse with nothing being done, when the girl and the vampire can't fuck because he might accidently kill her if they do. It's so hot.

Once Gosling and Mulligan hold hands, or rather she puts her hand on top of his gloved driving hand, which is on the gearshift. That's all we get of sex until finally, two-thirds of the way through the movie, they're in an elevator in their building, the same elevator where they met, and a man beside them is reaching under his coat for a gun. Gosling turns to Mulligan and kisses her for the first time, really deeply kisses her. The lights start to glow and the electronica is soft and pulsing, and the kiss is in super-slow motion and lasts a really long time. Then he pushes her into the corner, smashes the man's head against the elevator buttons, throws him to the floor and stomps on his head until it's muck and blood sprays all over and the man is dead but Gosling keeps stomping anyway, like he wants to cover himself in blood. Then the elevator doors open and Mulligan backs out and just stares at him.

When someone changes that much, that suddenly, it feels like either the old version was the real one and this new one must be some kind of monstrous double, or if the new one is real, then that old version must always have been a lie.

The guitar player starts fucking another girl and suddenly won't speak to me when I see him in the bar across the street.

The tragic reversal makes you ache to turn back the clock.

On the other hand, the tragic reversal is already a time machine. It throws you into the past to see everything again but differently, makes you pose questions you can never answer. In the elevator, Mulligan sees that the man who seemed so different from her temperamental criminal of a husband is the same as him, just as violent or worse. So was she doing something different, in loving someone who seemed so sweet, or just repeating the same thing? She'll never know the answer, but it will probably bother her forever, unless she's the kind of woman who can just forget about things and move on.

My favorite residents of Williamsburg are machines of the tragic reversal, the kinds of people who always turn away and disappear into their secret lives – people who pose certain intense problems of interpretation, in a place where no street stays the same for more than a few weeks at a time.

This building is a question about how you live after

a tragic reversal, thrown back into history and wondering what can be recovered by returning to the scene.

It was the loveliest hangover I've ever had, watching *Drive*. Everytime I try to do molly again, though, the hangovers are so bad they make me want to hurl myself out these windows onto the Williamsburg Bridge just to make the hangovers stop making me want to die. But every next day I wake up resurrected, because this building is full of joy.

Drunks, drug addicts, sex addicts, compulsive gamblers, and/or people on or recovering from deep, life-threatening benders: these are the only people who really hold my interest, which means that I usually am friends with or fuck and/or love people with a dead parent or two, bipolar or otherwise depressed people, musicians, writers, and/or pathological liars. Even so, I never know when I meet them. They always just seem to me like the best people in the world. At some point, a week or two into the friendship or the affair, I find out, but by then I'm already hooked, because the things these people do to ensure they don't have to live in the straight world are wonderful. They turn ordinary nights into wide electric universes that snap in the head like a new beat, get and give pleasure like they'll otherwise die, make music what music is and art what art is. Because they cannot do all the things it takes to marry, they can bring a whole marriage's worth of intimacy into one night of fucking, and you can let that land square on you, like you're the only girl in the world, to quote Rihanna. You're almost definitely not the only girl in their world, but that's the thing about addicts: they are endlessly optimistic, and they can make you believe anything.

I am not unfamiliar with the reasons it is considered unhealthy to love people who can't get through a day without getting shitfaced. They get in stupid fights in bars with guys they think are hitting on you, and you have to hug them until they calm down and sneak your number to the other guy later. When you start fucking someone else, they come to your house in the middle of the night, wasted, and let all the air out of the new guy's tires. They make you stop being friends with all the friends you fucked before you met them, that's how much they love you. And yet they always turn out to be plagued by focus problems when it comes to you. They'll eye-fuck you all through their set and then sit down right next to you and start making out with your friend. They'll say they're not fucking the girl who fills your shared kitchen with baked goods every time you go out of town, until you make out with her boyfriend and force her to angrily admit they've been having an affair. There is the moodiness, the way they'll suddenly start shouting at you on street corners in foreign cities because they can't handle stress and they're too high to read a map. They'll steal tobacco from your purse on the way out of your apartment and then pretend they didn't know it was yours. They'll leave a stolen wallet by your bed and then break back into your building to retrieve it, and have the nerve, when confronted, to pretend that it's not stolen but theirs, and that it is you who has forgotten their real name and how different faces can look on government-issued ID cards. Not to mention how when you ask why their eyes are half-closed all the time, they keep saying they're just really relaxed and happy to be with you, and all the rifling through their shit to find the Oxycontin they say they don't have, the way that even when they're vomiting and slimy on the floor of the casino hotel on your only vacation of the year, and you're trying for three days to get them to eat even the smallest piece of room-service bagel, they still don't admit they're in withdrawal again, and you still believe they just have a really bad stomach, that they're just so sensitive.

The problem is that I find these ways of behaving charming – infinitely more interesting, somehow, than the things that sober people do.

I go out. In the bar across the street they are playing Kavinsky and Lovefoxxx, from the *Drive* soundtrack, his scratchy metallic synthesized voice singing: 'I'm going to show you where it's dark/ But have no fear.' I can start out arguing about geography with a drunk from South Carolina and fall briefly in love with a floppy-haired cokehead who's straight out of

Winesburg, Ohio and end up giving a blowjob in the bathroom to a French businessman, and I can carry all these people into the next day, each one stretching the regular world just a little bit. I can stay exactly where I am and see what happens, or I can follow some drunk or drug addict to some other bar or party in Bushwick or Bed-Stuy. Even in the hipster bars they are playing Rihanna's song about pill-popping romance, over and over: 'We found love in a hopeless place.'

There are things you will never know unless you follow these kinds of people around. Here is one of them: you can drink enough whiskey that the hangover feels opiate, and when you finally make it outside at twilight the next day, the world is soft and purple and shifting and the faces of the people on the sidewalk are lit up with possibility and mad peace.

It doesn't always work out. I bring home a wild long-bearded drunk who fucks me within an inch of my life and then doesn't call. I pick up a drunk on the street who says he works for the UN, and that he was trained by the FBI to establish perimeters during explosives investigations or something, whom I don't call. I see a dirty strung-out man on the G train platform with a canvas under his arm and the eyes of a pervert or a man on a cross and we share a look I will never forget, of recognition and sex and the exact shining thing I enjoy mistaking for love, but I am on the train, passing, and soon he is out of sight. Another night I try to pick up a drummer in a country band. He looks like

Kid Rock, and, if I squint, like David Foster Wallace, and I'm sure he means to come home with me. But something's off about him. I tell him he looks bored while he drums. He says his back hurts because he was recording all day. I don't think drummers should talk like this, especially drummers who look like Kid Rock, and I berate him for being tired and bored. He should be sexy but he's just not. It's frustrating. Berating him, however, does not turn out to be a good tactic for seducing him. The next day it occurs to me what was so off about him: he must have been sober.

How do sober people get close to one another? No one knows, at least no one I know does. In the movies, they ask each other out on dates. One person says, Do you want to hang out tomorrow night? The other one says, Yeah, eight o'clock? And that's it. They never say what they're going to do, or where they're going to meet. I worry about them wandering around the city, watches unsynchronized, wishing they'd remembered to make a fucking plan. It's so much easier to get completely wasted and just go home together that very night.

I've been doing this since college, and I'm not just in it for the rapture. I do the other part, too. I'm the friend who will let you crash in my bed for three days and nights when you're ready to go through the shakes, sit with you while you moan, try to get you to eat toast, oatmeal, anything, force water down your throat while you sweat all over my sheets. And a year later, I'll help you buy your week's supply of malt liquor in your New Orleans grocery store, pretending not to see the people looking at our shopping cart full of clinking forties, and my heart will be breaking, but I'll do it. I'm the friend who will walk with you down Metropolitan Avenue at a pace of a block an hour because you're so doped up and bendy that you have to hold onto each lamppost and mailbox for a while, considering, joking, nodding off, doubling over, until you're ready to move on to the next one. I understand that. I appreciate the way it slows down time. The way there's nothing for me to do but be with you. You make me feel very calm. I'll walk with you when you're so drunk you're screaming at me all the way home. How many times my job has been just to get someone from one street corner to the next, I do not know. I should have been a crossing guard. Because I do not say no, I do not say this is fucking ridiculous. Something in me just goes quiet and I'm right there with you. Later, when I'm sure I've got you, I'll say change, please change, but what I really mean is, look at you, what would you do without me, you're falling apart, you would fucking die without me, I'm the most important person in the world to you. Don't die. Stay with me. Never leave.

Repeating the same words over and over again, claimed Gertrude Stein, is the only way to make sure they will actually mean something different. I've hung a photograph of her in my bathroom to remind me, as

I'm putting on my eyeliner and getting ready to go out, that I'm supposed to be fucking girls instead.

I invite home a woman to sleep on my sofa bed. I know she is shy, so I am careful not to flirt with her. I make up the sofa bed, and then I make her an omelet. We drink Miller High Life and she lies down on the bed and curls over on her side and asks me to 'cuddle' her, and then I have these perfect, hard-nippled breasts in my mouth. Soon enough, I remember. Sometimes when you are making a woman come it's like you're trying to get her to sound like she's being hurt.

I can see the Gretsch Building and I know what's inside it but for the most part, when I look out from inside this building, the gentrification is to the north and behind me, like nothing ever happened. I write to the sound of the trains, fast and wholehearted. It's like I'm back in the neighborhood I moved to out of sheer dire love, like I stayed too long at the fair but I keep winning huge stuffed animals at the water-gun game. A loophole. Friends come over whenever they want, in the afternoon or when the bar closes, and we play music and lie on the floor and talk. We dance. I dance when I wake up, and before I go to sleep, and smoke too many cigarettes, and don't care.

It's November when the water turns off for the first time. For years, the building and its tenants have been in a legal battle over an endlessly impending mass eviction. I'm instructed by email to follow the pipes out of the apartment until I find the problem, without drawing management's attention to the fact that I'm in here, instead of my friend. But the pipes are always disappearing into the walls, and I'm too shy to knock on apartment doors. It's easier to work around the problem. In the old loft building where I met my ex, we didn't have a shower or stove for six months once, and we got by. As a child, I spent a month pretending I was Laura Ingalls Wilder. I'd wear a floor-length patchwork skirt my mother made for me and do my chores pioneer-style, the slow way, washing my clothes by hand and beating them with sticks. Sometimes to keep it interesting I imagined I was doing this on television. So I know how to handle this. I bring in buckets of water from the hallway bathroom to flush the toilet, fill up the Brita, line the kitchen and bathroom with glasses and Tupperware containers of water for brushing my teeth and wiping down the kitchen counter. I cart the dirty dishes out to the hallway bathroom and wash them under the faucet in icy water. On days when I might bring someone home, I walk down the stairs and a few blocks to the place where the messenger lives now and take a shower, shave my legs, press warm water on my face, and walk back, my hair wet in the winter air, past the broken elevator, up the six flights. There is less and less time for working and writing, but I don't mind. Soon the bathroom begins to smell awfully of shit, though, and I worry that the sewage is coming up, working its way up these six floors to flood the loft. After two weeks, the super goes down to the basement and turns the water on again, which he must have known how to do all along.

I'm in here getting all pioneer-style with my water, but it's pioneer style they're selling in the form of hand-spun woolen socks for $80 a pair at the general store in Marlow & Sons, across the street from the Gretsch Building. Even so, I cannot resist the happiness of being back here, in the old world, if I am really back, if one can return to the scene.

I buy a fake shearling coat like we used to wear in the '90s, a dark druggie coat with a big collar.

In *Paradise Lost*, it's Satan who thinks the mind can make a heaven of hell, a hell of heaven. He is, famously, the best character in the movie.

I just treat the physical neighborhood itself as if it is on drugs. When I look at it like that, I love it.

In Al-Anon, the doctrine of renouncing addiction to addicts is the same as the doctrine of renouncing addiction: the repetition is a symptom that the disease is beyond your control, that you are powerless in the face of it, that the antidote is to shift your dependence to a higher power, seek forgiveness, develop a moral conscience and some boundaries, put yourself into some abstract category – addict, alcoholic, enabler – and then, because you are powerless, you've got to leave it all behind. You can't go into the bar, you can't go on the internet and even look at the escort ads, you can't try to help your drunk of a husband or your crackhead wife. Instead, you have to weave around yourself this network of strangers who are in your addict category, exit the alternate world you made, go back into the dull real world you were trying to escape, and just take it one day at a time. It's one world or the other – though you get out through one small excruciating step at a time, and you must always and forever, from now on, consider yourself 'in recovery.'

Programs that reject AA for its puritanical attitude toward intoxicants tend to treat that opposition of worlds as precisely the problem. When you're trying to quit something, this is exactly the double bind: should you view the thing you're addicted to as so powerful that you need to marshal every weapon you can against it, as if it is some overwhelming, apocalyptic force of evil? Should you disavow as false every moment of total transcendence the thing ever gave you? Or would you by means of that disavowal be giving the thing more power than it actually has, and was that exactly the problem in the first place? You thought it was the drug or the person or the place that transported you, subjected you, dominated you, lit you up, disappeared you, raptured you, loved you, but was it really you all along?

The double bind is a fake, too, of course. It's not one or the other. These are the kinds of questions addicts ask, because they are impossible to answer, so we can keep holding on to them forever.

Drive isn't playing at the Nitehawk anymore so I go see it again at Village East. The sound is bad and there are no Bloody Marys. It's just a film noir. The city's shiny surfaces barely contain the violence underneath, and maybe Gosling is like the city, a dissembler and monstrous. When you know that for the last third of the film he'll be smashing dudes' heads with his boots and drowning them in dark oceans and shoving bullets down their throats in strip clubs and ripping their eyeballs out with hammers or whatever (I had my eyes closed), every early minimalist line, especially the sweet ones, sounds excruciatingly fake, like it's in quotes, like he's just saying whatever everyone wants him to say but just barely. Maybe the kiss is violent in the first place, since Gosling knows he has to steal it before he reveals his secret self. Even worse, maybe the kiss is a cover-up. He uses her, so he can catch his victim off-guard. I don't want it to be this, not this interpretation. It seems like a real kiss, a good kiss, but why does he want her to have the taste of his tongue in her mouth while she watches him become a vision of pure brutality, have the feeling of that perfect chest pressed against her (as Emma Stone's character says to Gosling in *Crazy,*

Stupid, Love when he takes off his shirt, 'Seriously? You look like you're airbrushed!') as she learns everything she believed about him is false?

Trying to figure out whether someone's evil or good is like trying to figure out whether cigarettes are evil or good. It's a way to procrastinate. They're just plants and chemicals wrapped in paper. You're the one smoking them.

Gosling is everyone's favorite male lead these days. He's everywhere. A friend said the other day, I wish Ryan Gosling would just leave me alone. Because he had most of his dialogue taken out of this film, it's easy to project onto his character the Gosling of *Half Nelson* and *Blue Valentine*, working men who teach public school and do construction while wearing impossibly hipsterish clothes. Men who look at their female leads with a kind of searching intimacy that will be shattered or cemented by the secret yet to be revealed: the drug problem, the drinking problem, the brutal temper that we have to decide whether or not to forgive. Is his nameless character in *Drive* also *The Notebook*'s long-suffering workingman romantic hero, quiet 'cause he's sweet, or is he the *Crazy, Stupid, Love* womanizer, sweet 'cause he's about to break your heart? The film's music is about him. Is he a 'real hero,' as the soundtrack says? Is he a 'real human being'?

These are the kinds of questions I'm talking about. Asking them is a way of not renouncing or mourning. This is the way to make the man or the drug or the place uncannily powerful, infused with one's own contradictory interpretations. To love what one has made magical, in this way – at least when it comes to loving addicts and the kinds of drugs that can kill you – is widely considered to be a terrible thing, something to heal from. But our favorite recent romance – 100 million copies sold and over one billion dollars at the box office – is about a girl heroic enough to love a vampire who stalks and bosses her around and is addicted to her blood. She keeps wondering: Is he an asshole? But then how can he be so beautiful? Is it possible that he's being an asshole because he loves her so much? In this case, love for the otherworldly addict totally pays off. *Twilight*'s Edward Cullen solves the elevator scene problem, rewinds the tragic reversal: his initial coldness and violence turn out to be totally explained by his own heroic efforts not to kill her. He loves her so much he feigns hating her to protect her. So in this case it's the sweetness that's the secret, the surprise. One reads these books like they're crack, or some women do. Finally, he turns her into a vampire, so that she won't ever have to die.

I keep seeing the dead body of my father in the corner of the studio, naked and blue and cold like a corpse in a morgue. In reality I have never seen his body like that. I've seen him naked and I've seen him dead, but not at the same time. When he died, in a nursing-home bed, I'd been sitting with him for three days, talking to him about our whole lives, not knowing if he could hear me, because he was in a coma, just talking anyway. For twenty years he'd been on a cocktail of drugs for diabetes and epilepsy that made him have moods that were always opposite of one another. My mother and my brother and I were always trying to anticipate whether we'd get the sweet or the brutal, but there was never really any way to know, and it could turn in a second. I couldn't blame him for the bad moods because it was the drugs, or it always might be; there was never any real way to know what was the drugs and what was him. It wasn't really fair to feel things about what he said or did. The most important thing was to keep him from having seizures.

As a child, when I wasn't pretending to be Laura Ingalls Wilder, I was narrating what happened in my head like we were in a novel; after someone spoke I'd say 'he said'; after I spoke, I'd say 'she said,' in my head where no one could hear. It was better not to feel things during the later years, either, when the epilepsy drugs took the meanness away, made him as soft and tearful and wild-smiling as a doped-up bum or a child. I sat with him for the last three days and talked to him about all this, and told him that I'd hated him because he was mean or cold as fuck half the time, and thanked him because the other half he was kind and wise and taught me how to think and how to be.

I was holding his hand when I felt his blood slow. I put my hand on his wrist and felt his heartbeats separate. I put my hands on his legs and felt the blood stop; there was one last thick pulse and then there was none. I put my hands on his neck and there was one last pulse and there was no pulse. As a child, when incomprehensible things happened, I used to panic, and my parents would give me sips of wine to calm me down. But now I was as quiet and calm as could be. I put my hands on his chest and felt him completely still, and I put my forehead against his forehead and cried onto his face. My poor father. What he would be doing back in the corner of the studio looking like a corpse on *Law and Order* I do not know. He's not a metaphor, a reason, or even a clue. He's just a dead body encrypted inside this new life.

I buy a bright red hoodie from fucking American Apparel and wear it every day. On the third day I realize it's yours, the one you were wearing every day under your leather jacket when I met you. I'm the drunk now, when I want to be. I'm the addict. I'm the one to follow around the neighborhood, the one who changes things, over and over again.

The building is getting louder. There's clanking in the eastern wall, sometimes the sound of a small dog inside the western wall. The water goes off, comes on again. Someone is banging on the pipes at four in the morning, but who would do that? Sometimes the clanking sounds like it's right inside the wall beside my bed, but it is not possible that there is anyone in there. Sometimes the steam heater makes the building so hot I'm opening all the windows, leaning out the window looking over the bridge in a tank top and underpants and burning my legs on the pipes. The real tenants are in court with management, fighting to stay, but the building is winning, they're going to build their multimillion-dollar condos, and I stop being able to look out the window without wondering when this will end and where I will go. I would like to decide to leave, myself, before they throw us out, but I don't know how to stop wanting to be here.

The second and only other time it snows this winter, I'm so high that I can't understand why everything is white. I'm taking a walk with friends, everyone alarmingly stoned from pot brownies, arms linked, and finally I announce that we should decide that the whiteness is snow, though I don't believe we have any real evidence for it. The pot had made it so that to believe in and state the obvious required a giant leap of faith.

That same day, on a long car ride, some of us were reading aloud Stanley Cavell's book on film and love and marriage, *Pursuits of Happiness*, where he talks about wrestling with the meaning of films as a practice joined to 'checking one's experience,' which he describes as 'momentarily *stopping*, turning yourself away from whatever your preoccupation and turning your experience away from its expected, habitual track, to find itself, its own track: coming to attention. The moral of this practice is to educate your experience sufficiently so that it is worthy of trust.' To have authority in the interpretation of your own experience is a paradox, he says, because 'educating' your experience can't come in advance of the trusting.

Loving a place that is always disappearing before your eyes, loving people who are always disappearing into secret lives, and doing this drunk or high – these can be ways of making it extra difficult to learn to trust your own interpretation. You can think that to come to attention means to get sober. This can be a useful thing to think. Or you can think that love and intoxication are themselves ways of stopping, abandoning oneself to the lush and impossible moment between experience and interpretation, where it might be possible to let what is dead be dead.

I bring home a cokehead chef who has to get to his restaurant early in the morning, so we decide to stay up all night. He has the face of a child and at one point he is on top of me and I say, How are you able to do this? And he says, I'm 25. (No one ever says, It's the drugs! They make me feel immortal!) How old are you, he asks. I put my hands on either side of his face and look at him. Older. I put my hands on his neck and I can feel his blood pulse while he fucks me, too gently, but it's OK. I put my hands on his chest, and his skin is warm and smooth. I don't even like him that much but I put my legs on his shoulders and I put my hands on the back of his thighs and pull him into me and all is well. And then, because he is young and can't say what he wants, I guess, turn over. He puts his hands on my ass and kisses my back. Afterwards I put my forehead against his forehead and feel his alien 25-year-old brain, here for the moment and then gone, on its way to work, and I kiss him.

These are the most singular, unrepeatable kisses in the history of kissing, the one in the *Drive* elevator and the ones happening in my bed these days, because they are exactly on the edge of what's already happened and what will happen next, how I have seen things and how I will see them.

It is important to know that there are things that end. Things you can't change with your mind or even your body or even chemicals. As spring draws near, the building wins the lawsuit. We're getting evicted, the tenants who have lived here for ten or twenty years, and the subletters like me hiding out in these labyrinthine halls. 'The last of the starving artists who colonized Williamsburg two decades ago and began its transformation into the hipster capital of New York could soon find themselves out on the street,' begins the article about it in the *Post*. It's headlined, nonsensically, 'W'burg has art attack: Hipsters facing boot.'

There's no chance of an appeal. My neighbor makes a banner to hang on the front of the building: ten homes lost! She's been here since 1994, like most of the residents of the ten lofts. It's not a machine or a dream or a crypt for her, just her home, made impossible by money. Police cars come, sirens wailing, to remove the banner. There will be condos.

This is one way to quit: wait until the bitter end, when you have done all you can to make the time machine keep working. You have learned its inner systems, improvised workarounds, carted in the water yourself, but it becomes harder to keep it alive than leave it. What they call hitting rock bottom. The final tragic reversal may be slow, boring, and horrible. The time machine has turned into a crypt, but it is not a crypt if you go inside with the body. If you must raise it from the dead again, know the power it has is your own: bend over it like a vampire, fire it up like Dr. Frankenstein. When you are able to stop, there will be a moment when you have to just walk out of the building. It's not that living will be the opposite of addiction now; there can be more life because you know how to stretch out time, more joy because you have practiced the art of reanimation. You are a professor of transformation; you just need new tools. There is no outside or inside to it, no opposition, no right way to go, just this new way of seeing.

And I do not mean by 'seeing' that this is a matter of the mind or the brain or the eyes. The best thing would be if you could figure out what felt good about your particular drug and do it in some other way, with your body, like in your bed.

I am thinking of the Italian. The first time we saw each other, in the East Williamsburg country bar where I was cursing out the home state of the guitar player town by town, he did not ask but told me that I should take him home. Big wild hair. Divorce bender. Massive quantities of whiskey. Naples, where he got very specific and rigorous training in how to boss women around. When I met him I was very scared and after he came home with me, I couldn't very easily stand or sit for any reasonable period of time. The second time, we began to play a game. I tell him, in the morning or early afternoon, that he has to go home.

That I have things to do, I have so much writing to do, so much work. This makes him angry. In anger he stimulates every possible erogenous zone on my body he can at the same time, like a violent scientist of my body, until I'm like some kind of retarded gangbanged cheerleader/Anaïs Nin-type woman, kind of muttering in weird high voices, and he's like, really, you want me to go home, and I'm like, yes, go home, and he hurts me with the pleasure of pretending I have no choice.

But everywhere else I choose things now. The third time there is, at some point before the leaving game begins, a tear coming out of his eye. A tear so singular I just look at him, because I can't help him, I'm just not interested in helping anyone anymore. I say, What's wrong, what is it, and he shakes his head, and I let go of it. It's not my tear. And no longer is the suffering of the benders of others my suffering.

The first drug I took was acid, in an upstairs room in my college house with four girlfriends, all of us naked and wrapped in sheets because it was a Michigan heat wave – 110 degrees and too hot for clothes in Eastown, Grand Rapids, the kind of neighborhood where when it's hot enough you can smell the weed as you walk into that part of town. When the acid slowed everything down, I was watching my friends climb out the window onto a rooftop to smoke cigarettes, and I started crying, terrified that they were trying to get away from me, and that they were going to fall and die. From what I'd heard there were going to be twelve more hours of this, which basically meant the rest of my life. Then a friend put her arm around me. I found my way to some edge, thin as a thread, where the panic turned into laughter.

This is the diamond of the mind, this ability. A lot of people know about it, but I didn't know about it.

From then on when the panic crept in I could just push over the thread-thin edge to the other side, feeling the way to joy.

Joy is the knowledge that the thread is there.

A thread runs through the middle of your life, and if you find it, the second half can be comedy instead.

A place can make you want to die and then you can turn it over into the sweetest thing. You can do this yourself, if you have found the diamond in your mind.

Addiction is sometimes the attempt to raise the dead by returning to the scene. If you can't yet abandon the dead, at least you can practice abandonment, and will perhaps in that way be on your way to finding the world.

Something like summer comes early to the building by the bridge, seventy restless degrees in early April. The girls are walking up and down the pedestrian walkway in thin retro dresses, the men with their shirtsleeves rolled up, warm air on freshly bare skin. All over the building people have opened their windows and a breeze is fluttering the curtains, scattering projects and stacks of receipts. It's tax time, but there are a few more days to put it off, to walk around instead in the pretty light.

It's Easter morning, and this year it's Passover too. All week people have gathered to read the story of the liberation of slaves, of plagues that purchase freedom, and to ask, as always, how this night is different from every other night. The occupiers from Zuccotti Park are gathering again in Union Square and so people are walking around the neighborhood in T-shirts that say stop everything. Everyone thinks addiction and being addicted to addicts is a terrible thing. Yet most of the people in this country, on this morning, believe in a story about resurrection, about a body that never dies because you put it in your mouth once a week and it takes you higher, beyond death and time. It's the structure of addiction seen as redemptive, and maybe it is. But there are some moments, and this is one of them, when it's only in letting what's dead be dead that you can learn from your body the resurrection of the mind.

I am less interested in zombie stories, though, than I am in this neighborhood's particular light. The thing I most want to tell you is how the sunlight is here, but I don't know how to describe it. It's obviously the same sun that lights the rest of the city, but there is something different about it. Maybe it's our lack of trees, or the reflection of the river, or the lowness of most of the buildings, or the supersaturated colors, deep reds and greens, the bright wild complicated graffiti. We don't have the trees of South Brooklyn, the shady corridors of stoops, the tall stately brownstones of Fort Greene or Park Slope. We don't have cobblestone streets. What we have is this naked golden light. It's a thin, big-sky light, kind of Western, cinematic. Since the first day I saw it, it has alternately flustered and comforted me. Today its particular quality will have half the people in the neighborhood drinking in the afternoon. By five or six, some of the couples will already be fighting on the streets, one of them wrangling the drunker, more belligerent one home, because there is always a drunker, more belligerent one, and one who needs to feel like he or she is taking care of someone.

At the moment, though, a really tall guy on roller skates is coasting down the long steep slope of the pedestrian walkway with his legs and arms spread wide and the wind in his fingers. He has the biggest satisfied grin on his face. There are always a few people a day who roll like this, on bikes or boards or even just running, arms wide, falling down the bridge into Williamsburg, in the pretty light.

[2012]

Nikil Saval

– Birth of the Office –

In 1958, the Herman Miller design company hired Robert Propst, a professor of art at the University of Colorado, to head the company's new research wing. The company was aiming to expand beyond its traditional realm, furniture design, and into realms hitherto untouched by designers – agriculture, hospitals, schools – and Propst seemed an ideal candidate: though moonlighting as an arts academic, he was in fact an exuberantly, almost maniacally creative freelance intellectual, sculptor, theoretician. He 'immediately began flooding us with ideas, concepts, and drawings ranging from agriculture to medicine,' Hugh DePree, who was Herman Miller's president at the time, told John Berry, a historian of the design company. 'It is interesting, though, that despite our mutual desire to explore other fields, the first project that attracted his continuing attention was the office.' Interesting, perhaps, but unsurprising. Propst, in his move from art and academia to corporate life, simply discovered what millions of Americans have discovered since – that anyone who works in an office spends an extraordinary amount of time thinking about the arrangement of offices.

Propst found that he hated the rigid furniture Herman Miller gave him; he hated the static layout of the office in which he was supposed to invent dynamic concepts; and when in the next few years he began traveling the country, meeting with white-collar workers, designers, architects, mathematicians, and – crucially – social and behavioral psychologists, he found he was not alone. The postwar explosion of office work, in the newly great corporations of America – IBM, GE, Whirlpool – had created legions of employees with good benefits, relatively short working hours, abundant vacations. What is more, they were doing a different kind of work. 'In the last fifty years,' Propst would later write, 'in the most dramatic contrasts, activity has moved from tasks of rote to tasks of judgment.' Blue-collar workers organized, went on strikes, and were subjected to vicious state-sanctioned violence. White-collar workers, on the other hand, expecting to be promoted from within their organization, resisted unionization; each depended on himself to rise. Yet simmering below the surface, and bubbling up sometimes in the darker novels and plays of those years, something was definitely wrong.

'Today's office is a wasteland,' Propst concluded. 'It saps vitality, blocks talent, frustrates accomplishment. It is the daily scene of unfulfilled intentions and failed effort.' Worst of all, it was failing to keep up with the times. Human beings were performing new kinds of work, giving birth to new forms of socially sanctioned desires. 'We are in an era of rising awareness of the importance of individuality,' Propst stressed, and the workplace needed to express this. Instead, bullpen offices were the norm – vast caverns of undifferentiated desks, office workers bowed intently at the paper piles or rudimentary counting machines in front of them, encircled by a corridor of offices where management presided behind closed doors. At best, workers had two or three thin, waist-high partitions, which generated a poor semblance of privacy and individual space.

In 1965, Propst's first attempt to remedy this situation failed. Called 'Action Office,' his design consisted of a large space, loosely defined by three or four movable walls. There were three desks of varying heights – one low, designed for sitting, another carrel for communications, and a workstation where work could be done standing up – thus encouraging a worker to move vertically as well as horizontally. But the movable walls, which were the work system's signature innovation, were too cumbersome and heavy to allow for the mobility Propst wanted. More important, the space was too vaguely defined for it to be widely applicable or reproducible.

By the end of 1967, though, Propst had made significant improvements. The space was smaller; the interlocking walls were mobile, lighter, and made of disposable materials; storage space was raised off the ground. 'Action Office II' was Propst's attempt to give form to the office worker's desire. It consisted of three walls, obtusely angled and moveable, which an office worker could arrange to create whatever work space he or she wanted. The usual desk was accompanied by shelves of varied heights and variable placement, which required constant vertical movement on the part of the worker – because 'man,' as Propst observed, is a 'vertical machine.' Tackboards and pushpin walls allowed for individuation. Intentionally depersonalized, the new Action Office would be a template for any individual to create his or her own ideal work space. The effect of the Action Office would be one of constant dynamism, as in Futurist paintings of cyclists and soccer players, except that in Propst's vision, the worker's motion reflected not some machine-like capacity of the body, but rather the ceaselessly inventive potential of the white-collar mind. Early brochures for Action Office II play this up – we see modular walls expanded to create broad, half-hexagonal spaces; tackboards are used to great effect, and the walls are adorned by hangings, maps, or chalkboards. Workers are in motion or constant conversation, some even standing to make dramatic pointing gestures to other workers sitting on high swivel chairs (which force them constantly to move between sitting and standing positions).

So it was that in 1968, Propst unveiled Action Office II and published a 71-page pamphlet that trumpeted the theoretical bases of his new design. Called *The Office: A Facility Based on Change*, it was a kind of Port Huron Statement for the white-collar worker.

In addition to voicing the complaints quoted above, it offered solutions. Propst's narrative of the office teems with high historical drama, centered on one key event in the history of labor: the gradual replacement of America's manufacturing base with white-collar work. 'We are a nation of office dwellers,' Propst asserted. The face of capitalism had changed; the office had become a 'thinking place'; 'the real office consumer [was] the mind.' Repetitive work, of the kind performed in factories and typing pools, was disappearing, to be replaced by what Peter Drucker called 'knowledge work' – and the new office was going to have to keep up. Propst noted that in the spring of 1968 – that fabled spring of Prague and Paris – the New York Stock Exchange, which he called 'the office-of-all-offices,' suffered a 'hiccup' when the manual machine processing required to run share transactions was suddenly and dramatically out-paced by the volume of trading, forcing the Exchange to limit its hours.

Action Office II received immediate praise from the office furniture industry. Herman Miller launched a nationwide marketing campaign to educate designers on the use of the system, simultaneously inaugurating an accompanying lecture series on the future of creative office work (for which Action Office would be the ideal work space). Sales initially were slow, but after a competitor produced a rival modular office system, Propst's concept was validated, and sales took off. The Action Office eventually became Herman Miller's most important product and an inescapable feature of office design.

Years later, Propst would know what he had done. His design proved irrepressibly popular: in the year 2000, by his own count, forty million white-collar employees in America alone worked in forty-two different versions of the Action Office. Yet they would all be known by the same name: the cubicle.

Several factors aided the cubicle in its rise to monolithic status. The first was a seemingly minor shift in economic policy. In the early 1960s, the US Treasury instituted new rules for depreciating furniture assets in order to encourage more corporate spending. Furniture was given a shorter taxable life (7 years), while permanent features of a building would have a concomitantly longer one (39.5 years). This meant that, from the '60s on, it became vastly cheaper to buy and replace office furniture and systems like cubicles, since corporations could write off cubicles, but not fixed office suites, on their tax returns.

Meanwhile, new offices were being built at astonishing rates. In New York, a onetime capital of manufacturing where many companies began to position their corporate headquarters, white-collar workers outnumbered blue-collar workers two to one by the end of the 1960s, and great office towers were built to accommodate them: fifty-four million square feet of office space were added in New York in the 1970s, forty-six million in the 1980s. Expanding companies, attuned as always to short-term financial health, found it efficient (i.e., cheap and quick) to adopt an existing design rather than tailor newly built spaces to the particulars of their industry and culture. That design, more often than not, was Propst's, which required little more than wide, wall-less spaces in which Action Offices could be arranged.

In the cities, existing buildings had to be torn down or comprehensively renovated to make room for the new open-plan offices. ('You would think the simple fact of having lasted / Threatened our cities like mysterious fires,' James Merrill wrote of these destroyed buildings.) In America's swiftly suburbanizing expanses, however, the march of the cubicle faced fewer impediments. Low, boxy buildings ideal for a shiftable labyrinth of cubicles could be built on cheap empty land. These building-boxes could in turn be surrounded by box-shaped parking lots that could collect employees from an impressive geographic radius. Meanwhile advances in fluorescent lighting and air-conditioning meant that architects no longer had to submit to such concerns as the need for light or breeze. Indeed the ease of designing these offices meant that companies no longer had to submit to such people as architects.

Inside the big boxes, things went on pretty much as before. Until the introduction of the IBM desktop computer in 1981, typewriters, adding machines, and carbon copies were the predominant tools, except that now these tools were stored in cubicles. This technological stasis helped produce a kind of cultural stasis as well; most commentators agreed that office life remained largely insulated from the political ferment of the 1960s and its aftermath. Bell-bottomed or no, the conservative uniform of suit and tie, with all it implied, remained in effect. The office worker still enjoyed a high degree of job security (especially by today's standards), and still tended to view himself, in C. Wright Mills's half-derisive formulation, as a solitary frontiersman who would rise through the ranks, or fail to do so, depending on his skills and fortitude.

Mills had predicted that the objections of white-collar workers ('rearguarders,' he called them, or 'cheerful robots') to unions would eventually dissipate: 'However widespread the prestige resistances to unions may now be, solid, long-run factors are acting to reduce them, [including] the breakdown of the white-collar monopoly on high school education; the concentration of white-collar workers into big work places and their down-grading and routinization; [and] the mere increase in the total numbers of white-collar people.' It never happened. Office work did, as Mills had predicted, become more subjugated to the needs of machines – and therefore more similar, broadly speaking, to blue-collar work – but this did not lead office workers to link arms with their brethren in the factories. If anything, because of what happened to manufacturing in the next thirty years, the psychological need to erect clear barriers increased.

What happened was that, in the 1970s, major American corporations suffered a crisis in profitability from which they would never entirely recover. The generous benefits and stable wage increases that had defined a generation would vanish. Largely through layoffs, American manufacturing workers would decline from a peak of 19.4 million in 1979 to 14.3 million in 2005. Unions would be broken, declining from about 35 percent of the labor force in the 1950s to 12.5 percent today. The aggressiveness of the new era was signaled by one government action, unrivaled in spectacle: Ronald Reagan's decision in 1981 to fire 11,400 striking air-traffic controllers, whose union had endorsed his candidacy for President.

Insecurity was creeping into the office by the mid-'80s – for instance, in 1985 *Business Week* reported that at least one million white-collar or 'non-production' jobs had been lost since 1979, because of the even heavier losses in what it called 'smokestack America.' (In a particularly grim irony that year, the *New York Times* reported that companies were purging their ranks of in-house business economists.) But the white-collar worker hardly noticed and continued to feel relatively secure. History, after all, was on his side. The economy – as Propst, Drucker, and so many others had promised and continued to promise – would become perpetually more knowledge-oriented. Machines and machine-made goods could be produced anywhere, because the actual manufacturing process had been so pervasively routinized and de-skilled. Knowledge, however, unique to the character of the ever more individualized white-collar worker, was best produced at home. Perhaps the office worker labored in a cubicle, not a cozy corner office – but he might ascend to the corner office someday, and in the meantime, his semi-permanent walls were better than the laborer's open shop floor, which seemed more and more like a dangerous no-man's land.

Then, on or around October 19, 1987, everything changed. The Dow shed 23 percent of its value in a day, and in the recessions that followed, white-collar workers – particularly managers and mid-level executives – began to recognize themselves as the targets of mass downsizing. Between 1990 and 1992, 1.1 million office workers would be laid off, exceeding blue-collar layoffs for the first time. In the ten days following the '92 election of Bill Clinton, the pace of white-collar layoffs quickened (General Motors: 11,000 jobs; BellSouth: 8,000; Travelers: 1,500; Chevron: 1,500; DuPont: 1,243). Every year of the 1990s, layoffs outpaced the speed and quantity of the layoffs of any year of the 1980s. And it was all in the name of good fun. 'Destruction, obliteration,' cheered business guru Tom Peters in *Liberation Management* (1992). 'If 'clean sheet of paper' seems too radical for you – well, whoops.'

Under the now inescapable rubric of cost cutting, corporations poured money into cheap systems furniture, putting more and more of their employees in Action Office-type spaces. Naturally, the cubicles themselves got smaller. Between 1999 and 2006, the average size of a cubicle decreased from 90 square feet to 75. In some places, they were a lot smaller: in 1999, the headquarters of then media mogul Michael Bloomberg had average work spaces of four square feet, a squeeze designed to increase 'collaboration.' By 2006, polls would report that half of Americans believed their bathroom was larger than their cubicle; indeed, one wonders to what extent the extravagant growth of the American bathroom, and of the suburban home in general, is partly a reaction against the shrinking of cubicles, where the owners of those bathrooms spend so much of their time.

Because of course the hours spent in these shrinking cubicles expanded, as workers tried (without much effect) to safeguard themselves against the increasing likelihood of getting laid off. No one knows exactly how much the working day has lengthened, but a few statistics are telling: 25 million Americans work more than ten hours a day; 1.7 million work more than seventy hours a week; the average American has nine to twelve vacation days a year (compared with twenty-five and thirty in France and Germany, respectively).

As they began to seize more of an office worker's time, cubicles would become organicized and domestified in everyday office parlance. Dense expanses of cubicles became known as 'cube farms'; the phenomenon of people poking their heads over modular walls to talk to their neighbors came to be called 'prairie-dogging' – though this practice gained a name only when managers became interested in suppressing it.

The office – indeed, the Action Office – became an index of capitalism's relative accumulation of misery. From the revolutionary spirit of '68, a space had emerged whose omnipresence and deadening passivity were without precedent in human history, and whose future no one could contemplate with hope. The malleability of the cubicle made it indispensable to business culture, as Propst had hoped – but it wasn't the cubicles' inhabitants who had the power to move the walls. What management embraced as 'flexibility' manifested itself to workers as transience, arbitrariness, and uncertainty, always delivered from above. The flimsiness of the cubicle's walls became emblematic of the white-collar worker's flimsy security; worse, somehow, to be imprisoned in those fabric-wrapped panels than in stone and steel. The universality of the situation only served to deepen the pain; if the point of work (apart from earning a paycheck) was to express – as Propst had written – the value of your individuality, then the very fact of working in a cubicle, that bland, atomized expression of the essential sameness of all white-collar labor, was inherently embarrassing. Why speak of your workplace, when it was just like everybody else's? Why speak of work at all, when it was – as the cubicle seemed to prove – everywhere alike? Thus the eight (or more) hours spent in one's cubicle joined the eight (or fewer) hours spent asleep in the realm of what was better left unsaid: even if you could remember what happened, there wasn't much point in telling anyone.

The rise of the tech companies in the 1990s, with their explicit reliance on the intelligence and innovation of their employees, ushered in a new age of rhetoric about the liberated worker and his liberated office.

When the largest tech corporations expanded in the mid-1990s, each needed to consider the benefits of closed offices versus an open-plan office with cubicles. Microsoft added more closed offices. But most tech companies followed the lead of Intel, which had adopted the open-plan arrangement way back in 1968. Intel did not pretend that the cubicle was a great place to be; instead, it pretended that it could foster an egalitarian work environment by insisting that even the staff of upper management work in cubicles, that there should be no 'mahogany row' at Intel. A reporter from the *Los Angeles Times* described Intel and its famously ruthless CEO Andy Grove in 1996: 'Here were cubicle dividers, and behind the cubicle dividers was a desk, a computer, and a man, Andrew Grove. And you looked at that and you thought, well, wait a minute: What kind of business is this?' Another employee, introducing Grove at an Intel Science and Engineering fair, said: 'Andy has nurtured an egalitarian culture at Intel. . . . We all work in a company where Andy Grove's cubicle – which I think is about eight by nine – is just like everybody else's.'

Yet Grove's was a gesture of pure irony. The cubicle may have come to *represent* the exploitation and unhappiness of white-collar workers, but the idea that those modular walls, those tackboards, actually determined anything was patently false. You could hardly be said to occupy a cubicle if you could leave whenever you pleased, probably spent most of your working hours flying around the country in the company jet, and earned $200 million a year. This was not, incidentally, a nuance lost upon Grove's employees: his 'egalitarian culture' led to the employee-constructed website FACEIntel (Former and Current Employees of Intel), an enormous bloglike register of complaints about overwork and employee abuse. A quote from Elie Wiesel headlines the home page ('There may be times when we are powerless to prevent injustice, but there must never be a time when we fail to protest'), and the joke was surely not lost on the website's creators that Grove himself, a Hungarian Jew, had spent the war hiding out in a cellar.

In the late '90s, the New Economy companies

made the related mistake of confusing the cubicle with the worker's prison, and its destruction with his liberation. Or maybe they knew just what they were doing. The anomalous Chuck E. Cheese's workplaces of those years – iconic sunburst-bearers of computer science like Razorfish (motto: 'Everything that can be digital will be') – announced themselves as cubicle-free zones of unbridled creativity. The workplaces were empty lofts and warehouses in New York's SoHo or San Francisco's SoMa district, buildings that still bore the traces (now refashioned as 'hip') of their blue-collar histories. These companies had relatively few employees, each of whom enjoyed, at least putatively, a measure of control over the company and his own workload. Their work spaces were sometimes like small neighborhoods or cafés, with coffee shops and fake street signs turning the whole area into something resembling the set of *Friends*. Above all, no cubicles! And free back massages! Enormous vats of colored foam balls!

In these fantasy camps, people worked 80 hours, 90 hours, 100 hours a week, and some of them weren't even being paid. 'White-collar sweatshops,' they came to be called, placing a slightly different meaning, suddenly, on the hip refurbished buildings they had reclaimed for the free activity of the mind.

At the height of the tech boom, Malcolm Gladwell reported on designers attempting to create innovative workplaces by basing offices on Jane Jacobs's *The Death and Life of Great American Cities*. As Jacobs emphasized the chance, organic encounters of public street life, these designers would make 'public' the private areas of the office – for instance, by moving all desks out into central, public areas. Constant encounters would encourage – it was a promising echo of Propst's manifesto – communication and potential for innovation. But the use of Jacobs hinted at a problem. Jacobs's neighborhoods, while succeeding on their own terms, could barely resist being overwhelmed by gentrification – their organic street life augmented with condominium towers, their working-class character devastated by the influx of luxury. What Jacobs could never predict was the caprice of economic management, and its role in the frequently ruthless exercise of urban planning. Seemingly organic neighborhoods were actually built up by policy decisions; their bases could be – and were – easily eroded, their inequalities exacerbated. So with the office, where control over the character of the place came not from the chance encounter at the 'street level,' but from above, behind the closed doors of policy makers.

In attempting to create enjoyable workplaces, these 'fast companies' failed to create humane ones. One wonders whether it was with chagrin or relief that their former employees migrated back into the cubicle farms of the giants (Intel, Viacom, Hewlett Packard) that had weathered the burst of the stock bubble. Of course the giants, too, took the opportunity to eviscerate their workforces. Beneath the gossipy media buzz about the creative-office revolution came the more insistent rumble of real history.

Two months before the Nasdaq collapsed in March 2000, Robert Propst died. Two years earlier, he had granted an interview to *Metropolis* magazine. Propst did not recant his ideas, choosing instead to disavow responsibility: 'Not all organizations are intelligent and progressive. Lots are run by crass people who can take the same kind of equipment and create hellholes. They make little bitty cubicles and stuff people in them. Barren, rat-hole places.' That wasn't the Action Office Propst knew. 'We wanted [it] to be the vehicle to carry other expressions of identity,' he said. 'That's why we provided tackboards and all kinds of display surfaces.' He had, of course, not predicted that those tackboards would become, above all, repositories for clipped *Dilbert* cartoons. 'The things expressed in that comic are the very things we were trying to relieve and move beyond,' said Propst. 'It was a Dilbert world even back then.' Instead, Propst had unintentionally produced the office's most reviled feature: the flimsy, half-exposed stall in which the frightened white-collar worker waited out the days until, at long last, he was laid off.

In May 2005, I graduated from college; a week after graduation, I was working in an office. It was a large publishing house right on the Hudson River, with an open-plan office so spread out that I often got lost wandering its halls, even many months after I started working. My cubicle, situated right outside my boss's office (he had a view of the river, as well as the Statue of Liberty) had three modular walls, one of which was extremely high, separating me from my neighbor to the right. Even when standing, I couldn't see her. Nor could I see my neighbor to the left, who had the same high wall. True to Propst's vision, my cubicle had shelf storage space lifted off the ground, and I constantly had to rise to retrieve material from the shelf. It didn't feel invigorating, though. After two weeks of excitedly playing around with email and tacking up pictures and poetry, I had had enough. I sat much of the day with my feet on my desk, searching the internet for more quotes from Mario Savio and the Paris revolts of 1968 to put on my tackboards (*sous le bureau, la plage!*). I started thinking about offices and how crushing they were. But where else could I go, I wondered, since everywhere else was an office, too? At night, I watched the television show *The Office* obsessively, often until very late. I woke up feeling bitter, eyes sunken.

A year later, after months of trying, I found another job at another, smaller publishing house, which put out better books. My new cubicle was poorly arranged, so that my L-shaped desk left a wide useless space I filled with books and trash. My boss's office was directly behind me, and I had my back to her, which induced a perpetual uneasiness. The company was deliberately understaffed: the books-to-staff ratio was twice that of my previous company. My pay remained about the same, but the overtime compensation I used to enjoy wasn't available, and, after a few months, neither was a corporate vision plan (my health costs increased by $1,000 a year, but my salary didn't). Instead of working 9 to 5, I now worked from 9 until 7, or later. When I couldn't stay, I took my work home or showed up in the office on weekends. Having neither the time nor energy to exercise, I deliberately ate less, knowing that otherwise I would quickly become fat.

Eventually, sick of overwork, I quit. That was mid-April. Two weeks later, I was broke. I started temping at a small private equity firm, which bought public companies, reorganized their staff and management through layoffs, and brought them public again, laden with 'growth' debt. I got paid as much as I had in publishing, but had less to do. I had no benefits. My cubicle was in a hidden office, and it was two by two feet. My bosses liked me, but they realized I wasn't doing any work – so they moved me to a larger cubicle, right next to a very powerful air conditioner. In the midst of summer, I brought a bagful of extra clothes to work.

In June, my (second) publishing boss took me to lunch. The intervening two months had been brutal for the company's employees. The publishing house had purchased an imprint from another house, and, as usually happens when such sales are made, had laid off twenty-four of the imprint's ninety workers. More layoffs were promised, and more came. The company's

CEO issued a press release in which he explained that the job cuts were part of a 'painful reality.' The industry trade magazine valorized the action, pointing out that in an industry generally resistant to innovation, 'change' of this kind was 'good.'

My former boss and I talked about this idly. She complained about her staff, declaring that she wanted to adopt the Jack Welch principle of firing the least efficient performers each year. She complained about her workload, and then, interrupting herself, said – nearly cried out:

'Want to do freelance editing for me? I'd pay you. I'd pay you money.'

'Sure,' I said.

She took me back to the old office to give me a manuscript. The whole place was under construction. They were moving the new staff onto the same floor, but they weren't expanding. To make new offices and cubicles for the incoming staff, many of the old offices and cubicles had been resized to about half their original dimensions.

I grabbed my manuscript and headed out into Midtown, ecstatic to be free of such madness once and for all. I would work without benefits and for slightly less pay, but in exchange I would get – freedom! Freedom from the office, its arbitrarily rigid hours, its air-conditioned nightmare.

Now I'm frequenting the cafés of New York City, enjoying my freedom. There are many like me – too many. I have to get up early in the morning to find a seat, which I claim with a valuable laptop. I'm afraid to get up to use the bathroom – the other freelancers might not steal my laptop, but they'll certainly steal my seat. As a kind of rent paid to the café owners, I order a lot of expensive coffee and sun-dried tomato and mozzarella sandwiches on stale ciabatta. The music is loud, and through the day it seems to get louder, particularly when I ask the café owners to turn it down. Trying to read the words on the page in front of me, I find I'm mentally repeating the chorus of the last song that played (*I made a lot of mistakes / in my mind / in my mind*). The internet access cuts out now and then.

Still, it seemed worth it – because no matter what happened to me, *I was not at the office*, and it's hard to convey how pleasurable that is. Luckily, I don't have to convey it, because everyone already knows. But as I wandered the streets of New York, wondering whether there existed some perfect café that would give me space to work, I began also to wonder whether this wasn't exactly the feeling the office is now designed to produce – whether my reflexive disgust at the sight of a cubicle, those hoary walls, those fake-wood surfaces, didn't fit all too neatly into corporate plans.

Office-design theorists (borrowing their notions from the virtual 'desktop' and Microsoft's 'Office') wax rhapsodic about 'spaceless growth' – in which offices no longer increase in size, but the number of employees does. Smaller cubicles are one way to do this – but another, better way, the way that gestures toward a future of perfect corporate efficiency (i.e., getting something for nothing), is to persuade employees to rent their own offices, buy their own coffee, provide their own air-conditioning, pay for their own health insurance, soak up their own sick days, settle for no vacation. But where would you find such suckers?

Who in their right mind?

Well, me, for one. Lots of people. The financial advantages that corporations achieve by employing a casualized workforce of temps, freelancers, and telecommuters are humongous – untold billions in unpaid rent, infrastructure, and benefits, plus the sacred gains in 'flexibility.' And they can only do this (without significant resistance) when two conditions are met: (1) workers have to be deeply dissatisfied with life at the office and (2) they have to conceive of potential solutions exclusively in terms of their private isolation ('Get *me* out of here'). The cubicle, emblem of both disgust and isolation, lends itself to both these conditions. The only way out of the cube (besides being laid off) is to become a freelancer; but the absent freelancer suits the longings of management better than the docile cube-farmer ever did. The cubicle shrinks until it disappears; profits per square foot become incalculable.

Just as Margaret Thatcher said, 'There's no such thing as society: there are only individuals,' one is also tempted to say, *There is no such thing as the office: there are only cubicles*. Over the span of my office life – from one cubicle to another, and from one café to another – I have marveled at its spectacle: the way some indifferent fate seems to apportion each of us a podlike existence whose grim passivity and hopelessness are without precedent. And to think it all came out of the revolution of 1968!

In place of collective farms, we have cubicle farms; instead of political action, an 'Action Office.' In this situation, the ranks of the exploited include not only the low-wage clerical workers of Wal-Mart's back offices, but also – though it sounds bizarre – the educated, often well-compensated professional classes. Banking industry Masters of the Universe, Silicon Valley programmers, 'Madison Avenue' ad-copy writers: no matter the amount of compensation, overwork debilitates their family life and health; the frenetic pace with which they increase profits never guarantees the stability of their jobs. Civic life buckles under the inexorable pressures of the office. So, in turn, does the office vitiate itself. Information 'hiccups' like the overwhelming of the stock market in 1968 now occur with alarming and increasing frequency. Our contemporary foreign policy disasters are chalked up to ignored internal messages or misplaced faxes. White-collar workers report higher levels of stress than their blue-collar counterparts and suffer twice as often from severe depression. Managers respond by cutting benefits and vacation time and by increasing working hours. Their jobs, too, are on the line.

For my part, at the time of this writing, I'm preparing to begin a graduate program in literature. My latest effort to escape from the office is surely a familiar one. 'Brains, Inc.' Mills called it – another extension of the bureaucratic office world. And I'll even have an office, though nobody will make me go there, really, and I'll probably never use it except for my weekly 'office hours' with students. I wonder what I'll tell them. Will I say what I'm sure they already know – that their papers don't matter, that their hours spent on a thorny passage of George Eliot's *Middlemarch* won't help them with their securities research, their ad-copy deadline, their pile of documents still left to be filed? Will I explain that, instead, their education, the same education I got, will turn out to be an absolute nuisance, a museum of alluring quotations that they can only pin to their cubicle walls? Someday, I imagine, no one will show up, and I'll spend those hours doing nothing at all, as I often dreamed of doing in my cubicle.

Next time you look out over any city skyline at night, consider for a moment that all those glittering lights shine from offices, where men and women are working their unholy overtime. Even when the buildings are empty the lights remain on, as if to remind the world (as if the world needed reminding) that the demands of the office never flag or wane. Look, too, at the daytime café dwellers, and consider how the chief rationale for their anxious roaming is their unshakable dread of the office. Think about the un- and precariously employed, all struggling to get into offices or stay in them. The classical notion of 'office' is the 'fulfillment of one's proper work' or 'that which is fitting' (Cicero). What this should mean, for all of us, is the ability to produce and control our own work, in line with the ends of a community we support and love. Instead we have a society of offices, in which we are asked to obey commands, to produce and consume endlessly by diktat in order to live. Our choice is to spend life either in a cubicle or scrupulously avoiding one.

To free ourselves, we need to change the very operation of our desires, which the office has duped us into accepting. Our wish should not be to 'graduate' from the cubicle to the corner office – that self-debilitating aspiration to become the bosses we hate. As a front of united office workers, we must not merely make claims on sharing out abundance (leisure time, pay, reducing working hours); we must make claims on the real mechanisms of power – that same autonomy that was promised, and perverted, by the cubicle. When white-collar workers join together, against the arbitrary claims and demands of management, to demand their proper work, the effects will be felt far beyond the skyscrapers and suburban office parks. Propst was mistaken when he lauded 'the renewed rise of individuality as a value';

the Port Huron Statement was wrong when it claimed that what a person now wants is 'not to have one's way so much as it is to have a way that is one's own.' We stand together or we fall apart.

The *entire* office now is the space to claim; the world beyond it, which we have never known, is the one to win.

[2008]

Alice Gregory

– On the Market –

SOTHEBY'S, INC. NEW YORK. 2009–PRESENT.

I spent the summer after graduation reading novels in McCarren Park. I had been warned that nobody was hiring and was secretly relieved because this meant it wasn't entirely on me to have a legitimate job. I could copy-edit and babysit and transfer money from my savings account to my checking account in prudent but relentless $50 installments. It was fun so long as it was warm out, but by late September it was too chilly to read outside, and I was running out of money.

A classmate from college set me up at Sotheby's, a company I knew little about. In my interview, I told my future boss that I had never been able to imagine an idea that could be best expressed by *painting* it. 'But,' I added, making exaggerated eye contact, 'appreciating art doesn't mean you can send effective emails. I can write. I can make your job easier for you.' This is the best thing to say in an interview if you are young and unqualified to do anything other than maintain a personal blog. I started three weeks later.

This was October 2009, one year after 'Beautiful Inside My Head Forever,' the most garish triumph by an auction house ever. For that sale, Damien Hirst consigned 223 new pieces to Sotheby's in London, cutting out his dealers Jay Jopling and Larry Gagosian. 'I was indoctrinated by the gallery system – that you don't do auctions,' Hirst told the *Sunday Times*. 'If you don't like the rules, change the rules.' The presale estimate was $122–176 million; the sale would bring in an outrageous $201 million, upwards of six times the previous record for a Sotheby's single-artist sale (set in 1993 by the Estate of Pablo Picasso). But even more outrageous, in retrospect, was the date: September 15, 2008, the very day Lehman Brothers declared bankruptcy.

What followed was a down year for the art world. In 2009, worldwide auction revenues were barely half what they had been in 2007. Ad pages in the September 2009 *Artforum*, the one with the depressing gray Sherrie Levine cover (the one still lying around the office when I started) were down more than 40 percent. But my October arrival coincided with a new and cautious optimism. Everything was taken as a talisman. High estimates intimated a return to glory, and retracted items signaled despair.

Glory won out, decisively: in 2010, sales increased by 60 percent to $774 million. William F. Ruprecht, Sotheby's CEO, earned $5.97 million, up from $2.4 million in 2009. The average pay increase during this time for top executives at major US companies was 12 percent; at Sotheby's, it was over 90 percent. This past August, as the double-dip recession strode firmly into view, Sotheby's proudly reported the most profitable quarter in its 267-year history.

It was obvious from my very first day that Sotheby's would be exactly as I had come to imagine it. As the elevator reached each floor, archetypes spilled forth. Tweedy men got off at Rare Books, preppies at Impressionism, former sorority pledges at HR. The cool girls got off at Contemporary. In their jewel-tone flats and blended eye makeup, they were the ones who most resembled works of art.

These girls seemed immune to New York's damning seasons, which always threaten to expose one's tax bracket, especially if it is low. The summer sun didn't melt their makeup, and the winter wind didn't mar their manes. They were driven in cars and cabs that were kept at a constant 68 degrees. At night and on weekends, they attended galas, museum openings, and brunches in East Hampton. But during business hours, they went on client visits, consulted on prices, and tirelessly secured property. They were friendly on the phone, enthusiastic about the art, and harder working than people who look and talk like that usually need to be.

Hired as a researcher, I was assigned the task of going through the catalogues raisonnés of the Contemporary Art department's top-grossing artists – Warhol, Koons, Prince, Richter, Rothko – and determining the whereabouts of every piece that had ever come onto the global market. The Excel spreadsheets I worked on each day (column 1: image, column 2: title, column 3: year, column 4: cataloguing, column 5: present owner) would serve to expedite the future searches of collectors, who might want, say, a big, mostly purple Richter from the mid-'80s. Sometimes a painting was in a museum (the auction houses hate this because it makes the work more or less permanently priceless). Other times, a prominent collector was listed as the work's owner. Usually, though, I was trying to track down pieces in anonymous private collections. Sometimes a city or country was provided, unhelpfully. Private Collection, France. Or more often than not: Private Collection, Liechtenstein.

There were many ways to gather this information: hand-annotated auction catalogues, holograph index cards, old issues of the *New York Times*, cunning questions asked in the right way to foundation archivists in good moods. The method was cobbled together, and success depended on both a high tolerance for monotony and a willingness to flirt. I laughed sparkling laughs and framed my inquiries as either massive or negligible impositions. Sometimes I apologized: 'I'm sorry, but I have a huge favor to ask, do you know where . . .' Other times I used a postscript: 'Oh, and just one tiny, last thing: I've been told that . . .'

Founded in London in 1744, Sotheby's is the world's fourth-oldest continuously operating auction house. In 1955, a New York office opened, and in 1967, Sotheby's acquired Parke-Bernet, then the largest auction house in the US. Once a Kodak warehouse, the present New York location – on 72nd and York, a block from the FDR – is a modern, 22,000-square-foot building. In an attempt to preserve some old-world charm, the Sotheby's website adheres to a European floor-numbering scheme: The About Us page describes the New York headquarters as 'a soaring nine-story glass atrium.' (By an American's estimation, there are ten floors.) The bookstore in the lobby has been colonized by Assouline, the French publisher of luxury monographs (*In the Spirit of Aspen*, *The Well-Lived Life*, *Veuve Clicquot Yellow*). Upstairs are six floors of collecting departments and five salesrooms; the main auction room (on the seventh floor) can seat 1,200. The tenth floor has a museum-caliber exhibition space and a café – both surrounded by a wraparound terrace that yields panoramic views of Manhattan. The lower floors are marble, and the bathroom walls are striped buttery shades of yellow. You would never guess that the building has bowels at all, but it does: they are concrete and buzz with blue-suited art handlers who all wear name tags.

Specialists, versed in both art history and salesmanship, are the most knowledgeable and respected employees at Sotheby's. Throughout the year, they arrange private sales between clients, but in the months leading up to the big biannual sales, it's their main duty to secure pieces for auction. Property often comes to auction under conditions that the specialists list with alliterative delight: death, divorce, debt. But in the end, the process by which any work of art changes hands is singular – there are as many reasons for selling a piece as there are for buying one. Specialists treat each acquisition as a distinct undertaking, requiring specific art-historical knowledge and an awareness of the current market for a particular artist. When owners are reluctant to sell, specialists persuade them it's wise to push the property at this particular time (an upcoming museum retrospective, a new Chinese market for a particular artist, an Arab eager to expand his collection). Collectors are people, with insecurities and egos of varying size. It's the specialist's job to psychologize his clients and devise ad hoc strategies that ultimately earn him a commission.

Once a client has decided to consign with Sotheby's, the work is shipped to Sotheby's at the client's expense. Contracted conservators inspect the art under black light and prepare a report that details any damage or past restoration. Cataloguers perform 'due diligence,' which entails securing the work's certificate of authenticity (if the artist is alive, from his gallery; if dead, from his foundation), checking the Art Loss Register (an international database of missing art) to make sure the work hasn't been flagged as stolen, and completing a High Value Lot review if the work is estimated at over $10 million. Once the full provenance is confirmed, the work is photographed, written about, and reproduced in the catalogue.

Meanwhile, the specialists have been looking for clients, listing potential bidders in an 'interest list' prepared for each individual lot of the sale. A broad range of inquiries count as 'interest' – it can mean cold calls about the condition of an upcoming work or a cocktail party conversation that reveals a collector to be pining after a specific piece or artist. Specialists also, of course, court interest – giving tips to collectors and dramatizing demand. The length and seriousness of the interest list is the private metric specialists use to guess how well a lot will perform, rather than the more empirically determined estimate.

On the evening of an auction, Town Cars begin to pull up to Sotheby's a little before 6 pm. Diamonds twinkle amid ermine, and accents are unidentifiable. Registered bidders check in, receive their numbered paddles, and mill around the front of the room, where property from the sale is displayed. Then they take their seats, waving to one another across the center aisle. Slowly, the room behind the chairs fills too, with registered bidders not quick or important enough to obtain a seat, but also with young gallerists, curious dad-types in sensible shoes, reporters, and Sotheby's employees. Actual artists are conspicuously absent.

The auctioneer introduces himself and the sale, and with surprisingly little ceremony the auction commences. The bidding begins below the reserve and jumps past it in predetermined increments, toward the low estimate and, with luck, beyond the high. There is a certain amount of artifice to the performance, since the auctioneer has a rough idea, based on presale requests for viewings and condition reports, of who will be bidding on what. Sotheby's specialists, from New York but also from offices in Europe and Asia, sit on each side of the auctioneer in frantic rows. They take bids over the phone – often international and anonymous. In-house bidders do not wave their paper paddles; they raise a finger, so subtly it seems destined to go unseen by the auctioneer, who is in fact invisibly alert to the memorized faces of potential bidders. When a final bid is set and the gavel pounded, a digital screen is updated at the front of the room in six currencies. A display case worthy of Ian Fleming rotates; the first lot disappears behind the wood paneling and the next lot is revealed. During the competition for particularly anticipated works, the room takes on the tenor of a ninth inning. When it's all over, everyone leaves more quickly than you would expect.

In addition to the Contemporary department's major evening sales in November and May, there are also two-day sales, which include many more lots of lesser value ($3 million estimates instead of $30 million estimates). These sales are edited for maximum theater: lots with the most presale interest are staggered to anchor the others. Lesser-known young artists are included side by side with 20th-century masters, and a young artist's work can appreciate exponentially after a single bidder overshoots the high estimate.

By the time a work made by a living artist arrives at auction, its creator has already been vetted by some combination of loyal dealers at reputable galleries, kind critics at influential news outlets, esteemed curators at venerable museums, and sought-after art advisers with wealthy clients. Once a living artist is included in a sale at Sotheby's (or rival Christie's), he has already been on the block at a respected smaller house, such as Phillips de Pury.

Such was the case with Jacob Kassay, a 27-year-old artist best known for his silver canvases, which look like planes cut from a cube of mercury. In November 2010, one of Kassay's untitled paintings hammered down at Phillips for $86,500 – more than ten times the low estimate and eight times the market price being asked at Eleven Rivington, his gallery on the Lower East Side. The price was high enough to shock observers, even though Kassay's career was already swiftly on the rise. He had sold out his first solo show before it even opened, an especially impressive feat considering the state of the economy. In the months that followed, his work appeared in benefit auctions; the NADA Art Fair in Miami; and group shows at the Nicole Klagsbrun Gallery in New York, the Gagosian Gallery in Los Angeles, and Art: Concept in Paris. There were rumors that the Pace Gallery – one of the most important in New York – wanted to poach him.

It isn't hard to see why Kassay's work is so popular. His standard medium – a combination of acrylic paint and pure silver deposit – creates surfaces that appear pristine and mirrorlike from a distance but upon closer inspection reveal textural irregularities and areas of oxidation. His minimalist influences are apparent (Jacob Kassay : silver :: Yves Klein : blue) and critics compare his practice to that of the color field painters of the 1940s and 1950s. The paintings are beautiful, modern, and accessible: anodyne enough for a decorator, but obviously enough aware of art history to appeal to those for whom the adjective 'tasteful' is anathema. By May 2009, the waiting list at Eleven Rivington for one of Kassay's smart and shimmering paintings was almost 100 names long.

Kassay did not directly benefit from his Phillips triumph, of course – only the seller and the auction house did. But Eleven Rivington responded by raising his prices, and those prices remain high. When things go as well as they have for Kassay, everyone winds up happy. But in other cases, the relationship between auction house and gallerist is more fraught. As the big houses more often flip works by early-career artists, gallerists bristle at this encroachment on their retail market. Gallerists are in it for the long haul, which makes them caretakers of artists' careers: their job is to develop those careers, and to establish relationships with buyers whose past purchasing habits show discernment and who, ideally, promise to donate their collections to museums. Gallerists will do almost anything to keep their artists' work off the auction block, where it is not only susceptible to buyers they deem unworthy but also to the possibility of not selling at all.

The great fear of any good gallerist is a mass dumping of one of her artists on the secondary market, because – and this is always true – when collectors sell at auction it means that cash is more valuable to them than the art itself. If the prices get too high too fast, there is nowhere to go but down, and a poor auction performance, even after many good seasons, can spell trouble for a young artist's career.

Once, long ago, a boyfriend taught me how to spot a cheap dress shirt. 'They're kind of, I don't know, shiny?' he posited with disdain. Now I cannot look at a broadcloth without squinting for sheen – a wrinkle-resistant treatment, a trace percentage of Lycra. And it wasn't long into my tenure at Sotheby's before 'good paintings,' like 'bad shirts,' began to announce themselves to my eyes.

Art pricing is not absolute magic; there are certain rules, which to an outsider can sound parodic. Paintings with red in them usually sell for more than paintings without red in them. Warhol's women are worth more, on average, than Warhol's men. The reason for this is a rhetorical question, asked in a smooth continental accent: 'Who would want the face of some *man* on their wall?'

Here are some more qualities that make a work of art valuable: it is 'representative' (it looks like – and was executed in the same era as – other valuable works by the same artist); it has 'a good provenance' (important people have owned it before); it is 'included in the literature' (critics or historians have written about it in a museum catalogue or book published by a university press). Adolph Gottlieb paintings should have sun-discs in them. Cy Twomblys are best with squiggles. When it comes to Ellsworth Kelly, the more 'totemic' the better.

The art collector both appraises and is appraised by the same two facts: his taste and how much of it he can afford to indulge. Appreciation of genius becomes good taste, which all too quickly circles back around and masquerades as genius once again. Art collecting, like high school popularity, does not encourage much risk-taking. Be certain that what you're purchasing is familiar and well liked. But as in high school, danger and depravity go a long way. Maurizio Cattelan sculpts effigies of popes only to macerate them later with meteors. The breasts that John Currin paints are nothing if not pneumatic. Blasphemy, pornography, hubris – these themes are par for the course in contemporary art. But while tastes might run more toward vice than virtue, economically the secondary market is still a parochial place. 'Contemporary art has become a kind of alternative religion for atheists,' writes Sarah Thornton in *Seven Days in the Art World*. There certainly is a lot of zealotry. And a lot of blind faith, too. Despite art's reputation for distinctiveness and originality, its value is established not by the narcissism of small differences but by the megalomania of sameness.

After a few months on the job, I was assigned a new duty – writing the essays that are printed beneath and between the reproduced images in the sale catalogue. Auction catalogues are printed on glossy, high-caliper paper. Like the September issue of a fashion magazine, the weight of an individual catalogue is a measure of success and a matter of boasting rights for its department – in this case, though, weight corresponds not to ad revenue, but to the number of lots for sale. The catalogue is devoted to color reproductions of these lots, with accompanying text and smaller images known as 'comparables.' Comparables can depict other works by the same artist, archival photographs of the artist himself, or images that bear some admitted or presumed aesthetic resemblance to the lot (a Cézanne for a Joan Mitchell, a Dubuffet for a Basquiat). In the back, after all the color plates and the index, are pages explaining bidding terms and tax laws, which are only ever flipped through by merely curious parties who would never bid at auction. People who bid already know the rules.

The essay copy is mostly a formality, but it plays a role in the auction house's overall marketing strategy.

The more text given to an individual piece, the more the house seems to value it. I sprinkled about twenty adjectives ('fey,' 'gestural,' 'restrained') amid a small repertory of active verbs ('explore,' 'trace,' 'question'). I inserted the phrases 'negative space,' 'balanced composition,' and 'challenges the viewer' every so often. *X's lyrical abstraction and visual vocabulary – which is marked by dogged muscularity and a singular preoccupation with the formal qualities of light – ushered in some of the most important art to hit the postwar market in decades.* I described impasto – paint thickly applied to a canvas, often with a palette knife – almost pornographically and joked with friends on Gchat that I was being paid to write pulp. Pulp was exactly what I was writing. It was embarrassingly easy, and might have been the only truly dishonest part of the Sotheby's enterprise. In most ways, the auction house is unshackled from intellectual pretense by its pure attention to the marketplace. Through its catalogue copy (and for a time, through me), it makes one small concession to the art world's native tongue.

With the exception of the catalogue essays I wrote, Sotheby's felt detached from the posturing that happens in Chelsea galleries and the gnomic garbage that counts for art-world conversation. Auction house employees don't invoke half-remembered poststructuralism or make inapt analogies. They don't have to. The prices speak for themselves. Sotheby's is a world unto itself, with a well-known cast of characters and a set of recurring props. Valentino, a longtime client, is just as burnished and brown in real life as in *Vogue* photographs. Works once bought by the downtown art dealer turned museum director Jeffrey Deitch were of course not actually *owned* by Jeffrey Deitch, but instead by collectors who hired him as their tastemaker. Out-of-towners affiliated with Sotheby's stay at the Carlyle Hotel, which is equidistant from the Whitney Museum; the Gagosian Gallery; and Sant Ambroeus, the café on Madison Avenue where auctioneers and art consultants eat their glistening frisée, topped with all things 'tri-colored' and 'slightly sliced.' Ursus, the purveyor of fine art books, is conveniently located right above the hotel's lobby. I can now identify a Loro Piana cashmere shawl from across a crowded room (a disproportionate percentage of men worth over a billion dollars wear purple ones). I learned which vague-sounding conglomerates were in fact very specific magnates and which consignors were rumored to be divorcing, or worse, broke.

The men at Sotheby's greased back their longish hair with some sort of unidentifiable shellac. In their well-tailored suits and leather-soled shoes, they looked like patrician vampires. A striking number of my fellow female employees were engaged – not married, but engaged. Something was always being celebrated – a birthday, a baby – and the break rooms were sometimes spread with red velvet cupcakes several times in one week. The cupcakes disappeared in fractions, the cream cheese frosting slowly hardening as, over the course of the day, one girl after another slinked by and, with a quick glance around, cut herself a slice.

It was soon enough apparent that 'Sotheby's girls' – like rally girls or Suicide Girls – are screened for a certain set of qualities, and though these are not explicitly erotic criteria, they are, of course, many clients' sexual preference. In Steve Martin's latest novel, *An Object of Beauty*, his protagonist, Lacey Yaeger, is an up-and-coming gallerist. She graduates from college and joins 'the spice rack of girls at Sotheby's,' an apt phrase for the sort of self-assured, voluntary objectification we all acquiesced to there. The entire atmosphere is flirtatious. The very cadence of a good auctioneer is teasing: coy with one bidder, forward with the other, pitting the two against each other in a charged battle of tiny tics (paddle up, paddle down). He'll dangle an index finger at a phone bidder on one side of the room, while leaning his bespoke-suited body toward an in-house bidder on the other side. He pauses theatrically, repeating a price again and again until someone tops it.

Likewise, almost all interactions between employees and clients were inflected with an 'Oh, you stop it now!' sort of kittenishness or a steely tough love. Telephone conversations with cold callers included some of the most retrograde propositions I've heard outside of *Mad Men*. That it was possible to be asked on dates by men we had never met, solely on the basis of our summaries of sale results, confirmed for me that there existed, in certain circles, an assumption that asking a faceless Sotheby's girl out over the phone was a safe bet. Thirteen-thirty-four York Avenue, as it turns out, is an unimpeachable provenance to have.

The Sotheby's girls, and the specialists, and the auctioneers, are nonunion. But the forty-three art handlers, who are responsible for the safe transportation of art to and from Sotheby's, as well as its in-house conveyance, are part of Teamsters Local 814. On July 29 of this year, when the art handlers clocked out for the day, with their contract about to expire that month, they received letters telling them not to come to work on Monday. Despite booming business, Sotheby's refused to negotiate. Instead, the company hired Jackson Lewis LLP, a labor and employment law firm known for their hard-line anti-union representation. Presumably following the firm's proposed strategy, Sotheby's offered a series of unappealing demands: shortened work weeks, cut pensions, the right to terminate 401(k)s, new overtime policies, and the formation of a group of eighteen nonunionized handlers that the unionized workers would be responsible for training. Sotheby's issued insipid statements to the press, referring to the company's 'long history of a constructive and cooperative relationship with the unions' and citing the 'fair and equitable contracts' reached in the past. By Monday, the forty-three art handlers were officially locked out.

A month later, the art handlers gained the support of Occupy Wall Street, who came to see the situation at Sotheby's as symbolic of corporate greed. Throughout the fall, protesters picketed the Sotheby's entrance, interrupted auctions, and displayed inflatable rats and 'fat cats' in front of the building's main entrance. When Susan Sarandon joined the protesters – clad in red sunglasses and a nylon Teamsters jacket – pictures appeared in the *Post*. On two consecutive evenings in mid-October, dissenters with air horns swarmed Union Square Cafe and Gramercy Tavern – both owned by Danny Meyer, a Sotheby's board member. The same week, art handlers flew to London for the Contemporary sales, where they greeted collectors with high-pitched whistles and provocative signs, emblazoned with images of Edvard Munch's 'The Scream.'

By November, in anticipation of more protests at the Contemporary sales in New York, Sotheby's implemented security measures that limited access to the tenth-floor viewing galleries. Normally, these galleries are open to the public, and the presale exhibitions are considered by insiders to be some of the best opportunities for viewing contemporary art. This year, admittance required a press pass or a Sotheby's account – or, barring either, a $5,000 line of credit.

On the night of the sale, November 9, more than 100 protesters 'occupied' the 6 train (perhaps pointlessly – not many art collectors use public transit) and flocked to the block-long stretch in front of Sotheby's.

They blew whistles and yelled mantras ranging from the accusatory to the epigrammatic. ('Shame on you!' 'You don't deserve it!' 'Art for the masses, not the upper classes!') Protesters who managed to get into the building took their seats on the marble floor of the lobby. Sotheby's security guards quickly stood in front of them to block the view. From the auction room six floors up, the din was inaudible. Though the stock market plunged another 400 points that afternoon, the Contemporary sale wound up bringing in $315.8 million, close to $50 million above the estimate. The total is the highest for a Contemporary auction at Sotheby's since 2008, and the company's third-highest ever.

There's been little negotiation since July, and according to Local 814 president Jason Ide, no movement on the Sotheby's side, despite many counterproposals. This seems confusing; it's unclear why Sotheby's would have taken, and would keep on taking, such a hard line. The costs of compromise with a few dozen employees, especially at a moment of record profits, seem rather low when compared with the potential hazards of bad PR, and of relying on inexperienced personnel to safeguard multimillion-dollar artworks. Indeed, the only party who seems plainly to be profiting from the ongoing lockout is Jackson Lewis LLP.

One afternoon in spring 2010, while copying endless images into a spreadsheet, I heard someone calling my name. I pulled one headphone pad away from my ear, allowing some sound to bleed out into the room. 'Yeah?' I said, peeping over the drone of a half-listened-to podcast. My undecorated corner cubicle was fortified by out-of-order auction catalogues on one wall and large, hardcover books on the other; piles of *Parkett* functioned as a sort of silencer. Sometimes the lowliest employees have the best real estate. A girl from marketing craned her neck around my partition. 'Are you Alice?' I stood up and introduced myself. 'Cute skirt!' she said with a smile. 'Come with me.'

The girl from marketing told me that they'd been trying to track me down for the past hour. A consigned piece was being photographed for the *New York Times*, and they needed someone – a girl – to stand beside it, looking up in a way that dwarfed her and made the painting look even bigger by comparison. They wanted someone 'smallish' – which most of us admittedly were – but also 'in black,' which I specifically was rumored to be that day.

The piece in question turned out to be one of Andy Warhol's 108-by-108-inch 'Fright Wig' self-portraits, which the fashion designer Tom Ford, who is also a Sotheby's board member, had acquired from the estate of the artist. Like Warhol's other portraits, the acrylic silkscreens are based on an enlarged black-and-white photograph whose contrast has been amplified into a sort of visual paradox: a topographical map without dimension. There are either five or ten Fright Wigs

(Sotheby's said five), depending on how you count them. The famed dealer Anthony d'Offay commissioned the first five-piece series from Warhol, but he found them so alarming he insisted Warhol try again with another photograph. Warhol completed the second series in 1986, just months before his death.

When it came out that Sotheby's had in some sense misrepresented the number of Fright Wigs (Ford's is from the first series), financial journalist Felix Salmon asserted in response that 'the entire business of the art world is built on opacity and information asymmetry.' Salmon continued, 'One of the weird things about conspicuous consumption in the art world is that for all that it's conspicuous it isn't *public* – outside the big public museums everybody tends to be very secretive indeed about what they own and what they don't.'

I entered the gallery, and saw Warhol's vacant eyes staring out into the empty room. As the title suggests, it really is quite frightening, and it was easy to imagine it egging on an untimely demise or functioning as a preemptive memento mori. 'I never think that people die,' Warhol once wrote. 'They just go to department stores.' And here was his face – huge, purple, worth millions – being sold at what is indeed more or less a department store for art, with perfumed shop girls gathered around, gaping.

'Oh, good. She's blonde,' said the photographer. I made a face at him. 'For the contrast.' He sighed. 'You'll stand out against the purple.' I followed his instructions and approached the painting, gazing up at it from a few feet away at a quarter-angle to the camera. I shifted my weight subtly from one hip to the other and pretended to see things on the canvas that I hadn't before. Standing next to the painting, I was a live specimen of powerlessness: in service of sums of money too great and too senseless for me to comprehend. 'Back up a little,' the photographer instructed. 'No, that's too much. Yeah, stay right there. I need you to look diminutive.'

[2011]

Philip Connors

– My Life and Times in American Journalism –

My whole foray into journalism arose from a misapprehension. I wanted to be a writer, and I thought the most important thing about being a writer was seeing your work in print. Becoming a newspaper reporter seemed like the quickest way to see my work in print. I was 18 and callow. What can I say.

I spent six years, off and on, and $60,000 at two universities to obtain a bachelor's degree in print journalism, but six years and sixty grand weren't enough, according to my professors. I needed internships – as many and as illustrious as possible. This is how I allowed myself to be talked into a summer job at the Fargo Forum by a professor who knew the managing editor there. I would cover the beats of reporters who went on vacation, one by one: cops, courts, agriculture, religion, et cetera.

Eight weeks into it, I knew I didn't have the fortitude to write against deadline, day after day, on subjects I didn't give a damn about – city water-board meetings, the travails of emu farmers. The managing editor kept putting my stories on the front page, but the thrill of seeing my work in print wore off pretty quickly. The only really interesting story I covered was an anti-abortion protest at a women's clinic, during which the protest leader stood and shouted, 'Fargo is a nice town full of nice people. But when people hear the word "Dachau," they don't think of a nice little Bavarian town. And Fargo, unfortunately, is known as the city in North Dakota where they kill babies.' I wrote that down in my notebook and used it to lead my story. It seemed like something the residents of Fargo would be interested to learn about their town over breakfast the next morning.

One of my professors had justified this sort of story by calling it 'Swiss-cheese journalism.' He said people will often stage events or call press conferences that are plainly acts of demagoguery, and although reporters generally have a duty to report on these events with a straight face, most readers will recognize them for what they are.

It's like Swiss cheese, he said. You hold up a piece of Swiss cheese, and everyone can see what it is. You don't have to point at the holes.

I was beginning to doubt whether I wanted to make a career out of holding up pieces of Swiss cheese. One Monday morning, not long after my feature on the artistry of local pet groomers was splashed across the front of the B section, along with big color photos of poodles and dachshunds undergoing various forms of beautification, I decided I'd had enough. One month remained of my internship – one month more than I could take. I skipped breakfast and went straight to a neighborhood sports-medicine clinic. To a kindly but perplexed nurse, I explained that I was with the drama department at the university. We were putting on a play in the fall, and in the play there was a character who wore a sling on his arm. Our prop room didn't have a sling. I asked whether she might let us borrow one, or, if that wasn't an option, whether she might take cash for it. She seemed to pity me, for some reason; she let me have the thing for free. I told her I'd stop by with a couple of complimentary tickets in the fall, before the play opened, and she looked pleased. I was relieved when she didn't ask the name of the play.

Half an hour later I appeared in the office of the managing editor, empty shirtsleeve dangling pathetically at my side. I explained my history of shoulder trouble, told him in detail how I'd dislocated it over the weekend in a game of pickup basketball, and informed him that I needed to leave immediately to see my doctor back home about the likelihood of major rotator cuff surgery. The old man stabbed out his cigarette and lit another, wheezing as he shifted his enormous girth in his chair.

Listen, kid, he said, peering at me over the top of his half-moon glasses. I can't lose you. I've got people going on vacation. I'm short-handed.

I'm sorry, I said, but I can't stay. I can't even take notes anymore.

You can use a tape recorder, he said.

I don't have one, I said.

We'll get you one, he said.

I can't type, I said.

Sure you can, he said. You'll just have to use one hand. Hunt and peck. Half the monkeys in this newsroom type that way.

Give him credit for trying, but I didn't budge. By noon I'd packed my car, having worn the sling the entire time in case a colleague from the paper drove past the empty frat house where I'd rented a room for the summer. I was thirty miles down the interstate before I decided I could safely remove the sling.

Newspapers were not for me; clearly I was a magazine guy. Back at school that fall, I heard about an internship program run by the American Society of Magazine Editors. It placed forty interns at forty different magazines, most of them in New York. I applied for the next summer and was accepted. I was ecstatic as I ticked off the glossies on my list of preferences: *Time*, *Newsweek*, *Rolling Stone*. I'd worked at North Dakota's Largest Daily Newspaper. I'd written front-page stories. Now I was getting my due. I bought a Manhattan guidebook and reserved a flight to LaGuardia. I should have known the lack of the words Harvard and Yale on my résumé would put me at a disadvantage. When ASME sent the letter informing me of my assignment, I learned I'd be spending the summer in Washington, D.C., at *Kiplinger's Personal Finance* magazine.

I almost backed out, but one of my professors

reminded me to consider my résumé – my future résumé. I spent the summer fact-checking lists of mutual funds, money-market funds, and tax-exempt bond funds ranked by risk and return. To relieve the boredom, I drank appalling amounts of Paul Masson wine – you know, the kind with the pop-off plastic caps that used to sell for $2.95 a bottle – late at night on the Mall by the reflecting pool with the intern from *National Geographic*, who became a good friend, despite my envy of his future résumé. Toward the end I even wrote an article for the magazine, a profile of a telemarketing entrepreneur, and although the managing editor told me it was a fine piece of work, it bore almost no resemblance to my original draft when it was finally published. This was an unsettling development: seeing my name in print over a whole page of words I hadn't even written.

I had one more crack at an internship before I left college, so I placed my hope in the pugilistic world of political magazines. I applied to be an intern at the *Nation*, whose leftist orientation appealed to my underdog sympathies, and despite the fact that I'd worked for the glossy capitalist press, I got the job.

Here was a magazine with substance, a magazine with an exciting history. It was America's Oldest Continuously Published Weekly Magazine, having been founded at the end of the Civil War. Its pages had been graced by the work of Henry James, Willa Cather, Hannah Arendt, James Baldwin, Hunter Thompson, Gore Vidal – a world above the sausage-factory hackery of the *Fargo Forum*, or the service-mag boosterism of *Kiplinger's*. I prepared for a glamorous, amorous season of rubbing elbows with the New York literati, engaging in passionate but casual affairs with my fellow interns, the libertine girls of elite Eastern schooling – my just compensation for having been trumped, on the ASME internship, by the boys of Harvard and Yale.

The condition of the office was the first bad omen. The window-sills were coated in dust so thick it might have been there since the magazine's inception. The air smelled vaguely of unwashed underarm and cigarettes, and moldering paper lay everywhere in piles. Thankfully, the production assistant had the good sense to smoke his daily, fragrant joint in the men's room, where a perpetually leaking pipe kept the humidity high and the fire danger low.

When I showed up the first day wearing a tie, wanting to make a good impression, everyone looked at me nervously, as if I might be a poorly disguised FBI agent. I spent the next four months hunched over a telephone in a windowless room we called the bullpen, fact-checking articles on how to reinvigorate the labor movement, a longtime staple of *Nation* reportage whose frequency and desperation of tone increased as union membership declined. For variety, I did research for a contrarian columnist on 'the hoax of global warming,' but occasionally I avoided the research by acting as the columnist's courier – dropping off film of him and his girlfriend in racy poses, picking up the prints, and mailing them to him in a plain manila envelope. Those tawdry four-by-sixes were the only element of those months that could be considered vaguely amorous, although they didn't do much for me.

The hundred-dollar-a-week intern stipend matched exactly the cost of my sublet room in Queens. With a six-hundred-dollar cash advance on my very first credit card, I was left with fifty dollars a week for food, coffee, and subway fare. Mostly, I passed my evenings writing long, lugubrious letters to friends about the irony of working as an indentured slave for a magazine founded by abolitionists. The girls of elite Eastern schooling were more interested in guys who could discourse with easy intimacy on the works of Habermas and Derrida; an earnest Midwesterner with firsthand knowledge of techniques in pig castration did not exactly set their loins aquiver, at least not with desire. I missed my one chance to mingle with Kurt Vonnegut and E. L. Doctorow when I called in sick the day the interns were enlisted to serve hors d'oeuvres at a fundraising dinner for the magazine, which had lost money 132 years running. I very much doubted Vonnegut would want to discuss with me the bombing of Dresden while I held a tray of stuffed dates wrapped in prosciutto. I counted the days till I could return to school in Montana.

I did get one break just before I left. One of my weekly duties involved opening all the packages sent to the literary editors, an unceasing wave of review copies of the latest books, and on one such occasion I came across a book about a cyanide heap-leach gold mine a company had proposed near the headwaters of the Blackfoot River in Montana. I knew the Blackfoot well and agreed with the author that the mine would be a disaster, so I proposed an essay on the book and the mine, and the literary editor accepted it. Back in Missoula that winter, after the piece appeared, I waited for the phone to ring, thinking that now all the important editors in New York would be aware of what a stylish writer I was. When the phone remained mum for several weeks, I let my service lapse. The silence was too depressing, and I was too broke to pay the bill. If they wanted to find me they could write a letter to the *Nation* and have it forwarded, like people did in the old days.

After graduation I stayed on in Missoula, where I paid $180 a month for a studio apartment above a downtown movie theater. On summer days fishermen cast their flies upstream from the Higgins Avenue Bridge, seventy-five yards from my window, and a bagpiper went through his mournful musical paces, using the bridge abutments as acoustic enhancement. Mornings I eked out a living baking bread alongside a failed novelist who'd mastered the texture of the baguette, though not the art of fiction, during two years in Paris in the 1970s. Afternoons I worked on what I hoped would become my own first novel, an imitation of Paul Auster's *New York Trilogy* that stalled forever at forty pages. For a time I felt sort of authentically bohemian pounding on my old Olivetti while the muffled sound track to that week's feature film droned through the floor. The building's manual elevator, one of the few of its kind still in operation west of the Mississippi, was staffed by a woman who'd never abandoned the apartment upstairs where her husband had blown his brains out a decade earlier. More than once I heard a rumor that David Lynch had spent some time around the place during his stay in Missoula, long enough to use it as a model for the apartment building in *Blue Velvet*.

I'd finally given up on journalism. I wanted to devote myself to art, to real writing, to an eccentric vision along the lines of David Lynch. I might have been content to live for years hand-to-mouth in that heady mixture of squalor and beauty, within walking distance of eleven bars, had an old flame not dropped back into my life.

We'd broken up a few years earlier; she'd moved to Paris, and I hadn't seen her since. When she wrote to say she was coming to Montana for a cousin's wedding, we planned to meet for one last bittersweet romantic good-bye.

We drove through the mountains, camped by an alpine lake, and, gripped by sentimentality, agreed to try again: she'd leave Paris, I'd leave Montana. We'd meet in the middle, New York. I guess we had to prove to ourselves, once and for all, that we weren't meant to be. Which of course we did. One gray morning I woke up and found myself alone in a Hell's Kitchen sublet with the owner's four cats, wondering how I was ever going to pay my bills. Journalism beckoned.

I sent my résumé to dozens of magazines and waited to hear back, but in the end only one of them called me for an interview. I only got the interview because I knew someone who knew someone at the magazine. It was called *Civilization* and was affiliated with the Library of Congress. The magazine was glossy but kind of boring. I didn't care. I'd been in the city for two months and was buying groceries with my credit card.

I showed up in a jacket and tie and tried my best to look like a diligent and respectable young college graduate from the American Middle West. I was shown to the office of the editor, a man named Nelson Aldrich, who asked me about my various internships. I told him about all the intrepid reporting I'd done at the *Fargo Forum*, the article I'd written for the *Nation*, the many things I'd learned about the ways of the world while staring into the abyss of an impending deadline. I tried to make it sound as if I were the prairie incarnation of H. L. Mencken and no doubt went too far, because Nelson Aldrich immediately said I was overqualified for the job. He was looking for an editorial assistant. I told him I really wanted the job. He said I'd probably find it boring and he didn't want a bored assistant moping around the office. I told him I didn't mope. He said the pay was poor and I could find something better. I told him I'd already been looking for two months and didn't share his optimism. We spent most of the interview in this way, me begging in an unseemly manner for the job, him trying to talk me out of wanting it.

I'd done some research about Nelson Aldrich before I arrived for the interview. In addition to helping found the *Paris Review*, he'd written a book called *Old Money*, about growing up in a family that had a lot of it. I wanted to tell him that I'd grown up in a family that had hardly any of it, that I needed a job to begin paying my student loans and my extortionate New York rent, that if he hired me I'd be the most attentive and responsible editorial assistant he'd ever known, and that even if I became bored I'd pretend I wasn't, because I just wanted money – new, old, crisp, soiled, I didn't care. But he was from old money, and I figured he didn't understand such things, so I didn't bring them up, and he didn't hire me, and after I left his office I never spoke to him again.

I may have had to leave the city in disgrace if I hadn't called the former head of the journalism department at the University of Montana, a man named Frank Allen. He'd once worked at the *Wall Street Journal* and knew a lot of people in New York. When I called him, he gave me the name of a woman at the *Wall Street Journal* and told me I should call her and ask her to coffee. The idea was she might know people who knew other people who might want to hire a hungry young journalist from the northern Plains.

The woman was the newspaper's legal editor. I called her, and we met for coffee. She said, in her gravelly Brooklyn accent, that Frank Allen had hired her when he was chief of the Philadelphia bureau of the *Wall Street Journal*, and for that she was eternally grateful. There was no longer a Philadelphia bureau of the *Wall Street Journal*, and about that she was sad.

As luck would have it, she said, I've just been given permission by my boss to hire a news assistant. Would you be interested in the job?

I said, Yes, absolutely.

She told me to send her six samples of my writing by the end of the week.

I told her I would.

When I left the interview, which I hadn't even known was going to be an interview, I was conflicted. All of a sudden, I had a chance to get a job at a place that considered itself the World's Most Important Publication, but I didn't want to work at the world's most important publication. In fact, I'd hardly ever read it; I thought it was a fusty rag for middle-aged bankers, as predictable in its celebration of capitalism as *Pravda* had been in its defense of Communism. My politics at the time were fierce and not always coherent, but if they were given a one-word description I suppose you'd call them socialist. And while socialism taking root in America was about as likely as a manned space flight to Pluto, journalism, I thought, might at least be a means to afflict the comfortable and comfort the afflicted, as one of my professors liked to say. The *Wall Street Journal* seemed about the least likely place in the world where a writer could do that.

Soon I decided my politics mattered less than the anemic balance in my checking account – and then I realized I had an even bigger problem. The legal editor had wanted to see six samples of my writing – six – but I had only four or five really good ones from the *Fargo Forum*. The best thing I'd written was the essay on the Blackfoot River in the *Nation*. As fate would have it, I'd said an unkind thing about the *Wall Street Journal* in that piece. In reference to a logging company whose clear-cuts of healthy forest had fouled the river with silt and killed untold numbers of fish, I'd written: 'Even a newspaper as sympathetic to corporate plunder as the *Wall Street Journal* once called Plum Creek the "Darth Vader of the [timber] industry."' I doubted that the legal editor thought of her employer as sympathetic to corporate plunder, and I very much doubted that she would hire me if she discovered I'd written such a thing.

You can see my quandary.

Soon, though, I thought of a solution. I still had friends at the *Nation*, and I called one of them, explained my situation, and asked if he'd do me a giant favor. Would he go into the electronic archives of the magazine and touch up the article that said unkind things about the *Wall Street Journal*, and then print for me a copy of the doctored article, which would no longer say unkind things? At first he was reluctant. He didn't want to tinker with the historical record of the magazine. I told him he should of course change back my wording before saving and closing the file.

In the end he capitulated, and I sent a copy of the doctored article to the legal editor. She was impressed by it, and I was hired.

When I showed up for work that first day, on Liberty Street in Manhattan, just across the West Side Highway from the World Trade Center towers, in World Financial Center building number one, I had my picture taken and affixed to a little magnetic pass card. When waved in front of a laserlike beam of discerning red light, the pass card unlocked doors for me in the paper's austere corridors. My qualms about working for the bible of American capitalism were in quick retreat. I felt proud, powerful, important: I was going places.

I'd been hired as a news assistant. I thought this meant I'd help with the gathering and writing of news. In practice, this meant I fetched faxes and replenished water coolers. I spent most of each day standing over a squadron of a half-dozen fax machines, manually collating and stapling press releases and court documents, then delivering them to reporters who covered corporate law, telecommunications, and the pharmaceutical industry. I performed this task with actuarial efficiency, the paper a blur in my hand like a magician's trick; I served the reporters their faxes with the cordial discretion of a waiter in a fancy restaurant. My only means of discriminating good days from bad was by noting, at the end of my shift, whether I'd avoided a paper cut.

All day long I inhaled the hot ink fumes wafting from the fax machines. I felt an irrational fear that the fumes might have some secret, insidious effect – hastening the onset of lung cancer, shrinking my testicles. My job was pointless. I'd spent the prime years of my education working menial jobs and borrowing heavily to pay for a college degree that qualified me for a position that was already obsolete. Al Gore had invented the internet. People didn't need to send faxes anymore. They could send e-mail. But they went on sending faxes on paper, laying waste to great swaths of forest, enriching pulp mills and timber companies. I thought about mentioning this to my boss: Why don't we encourage people to rechannel their communications electronically, saving the world lots of trees and me lots of time? But then I wondered whether that would result in me losing my job, whereupon I'd be forced to wait tables at a tapas bar. So I kept my mouth shut and sorted and stapled the faxes, and cashed my check every two weeks, which still came quaintly on paper, despite the invention of direct deposit.

Once in a while I came across an amusing press release, which I tucked in a folder marked 'GREATEST HITS OF PUBLIC RELATIONS.'

New York University Medical Center: FOR IMMEDIATE RELEASE: NEW YORK, NY (November 29, 1999) – FREQUENT NIGHTTIME BATHROOM VISITS AFFECT SLEEP AND QUALITY OF LIFE. . . .

THE AYN RAND INSTITUTE – October 20, 1999. FOR IMMEDIATE RELEASE: FIFTH ANNIVERSARY OF AMERICORPS = FIVE YEARS OF SACRIFICE. Marina Del Ray, CA – The AmeriCorps should be abolished, said the director of communications for the Ayn Rand Institute. 'The AmeriCorps aims to indoctrinate young people into a life of sacrificing to society,' said Scott McConnell. 'That is a recipe for slavery, not freedom.' . . . Since 1997, the Ayn Rand Institute has been the only voice morally opposing volunteerism. Through the Institutute's Anti-Servitude Internship Program, students have the opportunity to fulfill their school's volunteer requirements by working to abolish volunteerism.

NEWS: Re: *PEOPLE MAGAZINE*'S TRIBUTE ISSUE RELEASE. July 22, 1999. Please note that there was an error in the press release forwarded to you this morning: JOHN F. KENNEDY JR. WAS PEOPLE'S 'SEXIEST MAN ALIVE' IN 1988 (NOT 1998). We regret the error.

March 30, 1999: FOR IMMEDIATE RELEASE: News from State Senator Roy M. Goodman: SENATOR GOODMAN URGES PASSAGE OF LEGISLATION TO REGULATE SPERM RETRIEVAL FROM DEAD MEN.

One day, about eight months after I was hired, I learned of a job opening on the Leisure & Arts page. It was listed on the company's internal website, a copy-editing job, repairing split infinitives and run-on sentences and the like. I figured I could do that. More important, I knew the job would double my salary and probably halve my chances of lung cancer. I had my résumé and cover letter polished by the end of the day.

I was confident of my chances until I learned that, in order to get the job, I would have to sit for an interview with Bob Bartley, the editorial-page editor of the paper, who also oversaw hiring for the Leisure & Arts page, which he otherwise supervised with benign neglect. Bob Bartley, who has since passed away, was among the most influential American journalists of the second half of the 20th century, although his name was not widely known outside of New York and Washington. He was fairly soft-spoken, and his posture was poor. He rarely smiled, but when he did he looked like a cat who'd just swallowed your canary.

His abiding obsessions were taxes and weapons. He thought taxes should be cut always and everywhere, except for poor people, and he thought America should build as many weapons as possible. The more weapons we had, in his view, the less likely we were to need them. But he believed that occasionally we might need them to bomb other nations that were trying to get them too, because those nations couldn't be trusted not to use them, the way we could. In order to further thwart the nations that, unlike us, couldn't be trusted not to use their weapons, he thought we should spend however many trillions it took to build a missile-defense shield, that sci-fi sort of umbrella that would protect America from the rain of other nations' missiles. (I always admired the childish simplicity of the concept: like one man shooting a bullet at another man, and instead of the second man shooting back at the first man, he shoots a bullet at the first man's bullet. That way, no one dies. Only bullets die.) Bob Bartley believed that with tax cuts, lots of weapons, and a missile-defense shield, Americans would remain safe, happy, and prosperous.

Bob Bartley had been writing editorials about these ideas for more than thirty years.

Someone once made a joke about editorial writers. Why is writing an editorial like pissing yourself in a blue serge suit? Because it gives you a warm feeling, and nobody notices what you've done.

Bob Bartley was no trouser-wetter, though. From what I could discern, he never had warm feelings, and people in power tended to notice what he wrote. The arena in which he'd had his greatest influence was tax policy. He was a ceaseless proponent of trickle-down economics: by cutting taxes for rich people and raising them for poor people, he argued, more money would end up in the hands of not only rich people but, because the rich people would spend it on maids and yachts, in the hands of people who cleaned houses and sanded the decks of yachts. Because everyone would be making more money, the government would generate more money in taxes, even though the top tax rates were lower. Since bloating the government with more taxpayer money was actually a bad thing, an evil outcome of good policy (I know, I know, it all gets very confusing), the government would be obliged to funnel the extra tax revenues to bomb-building projects – in effect throwing the money away, since it created wealth, in the form of weapons, that could only be used once, if at all, and then only to destroy, never to create more wealth, which was supposed to be the essence of capitalism, wealth creating wealth – while at the same time cutting programs for poor people, which would make the poor people angry at the government and entice them to vote for Republicans, just like the rich people did, ensuring Republican rule forever.

Despite the baroque strangeness of some of his ideas, Bob Bartley had once won a Pulitzer Prize.

When I first joined the paper, Bob Bartley was in the late, hysterical stages of his obsession with Bill Clinton. Bob Bartley's editorial page had printed enough editorials about Whitewater to fill 3,000 pages in six thick anthologies (now available on CD-ROM!).

Bob Bartley was proud of these books, even though no one read them. He thought Whitewater was comparable to Watergate; he was hoping to bring down a president, like Woodward and Bernstein had, and win another Pulitzer Prize. But despite his 3,000 pages of editorials, Whitewater ultimately degenerated into an ontological squabble about whether fellatio is actually sex, and the president did not resign and was not forced from office, although Bob Bartley was adamant that he should have been, because Bob Bartley did not approve of extramarital fellatio. At least not for Democrats. When a reporter asked him whether he would've attacked Newt Gingrich or another prominent Republican faced with similar charges of sexual misconduct, Bob Bartley admitted that, 'We would have defended them. That's the way it is.'

I was nervous when I went to Bob Bartley's office for my interview. My internship at the *Nation* featured prominently on my résumé. While the work I did there was utterly harmless to the spread of corporate capitalism – fact-checking articles on a labor movement that was doomed no matter what anyone said; researching articles on 'the hoax of global warming,' which Bob Bartley agreed was a hoax – the *Nation* was known to say kind things about socialists. Bob Bartley detested socialists.

Bob Bartley held my résumé in his hands. I feared he would ask me about socialism, taxes, trickle-down economics. Then I would face a choice: I could either tell him what I thought about these things, whereupon he would refuse to hire me to work on the Leisure & Arts page, or I could betray my own principles, barter away my soul, and lie. I'd been here before, and I knew which path I'd choose.

He did not ask me about any of these things. We talked about Minnesota and Iowa, where, it turned out, we had both lived as boys. He'd been born in southwestern Minnesota but grew up mostly in Ames, Iowa, while I'd been born in Ames, Iowa, and grew up mostly in southwestern Minnesota. This seemed apt, our moving in opposite directions at the beginning of our lives – me upward and to the left on the map, him downward and to the right.

Bob Bartley asked me only one serious question, with two leading follow-ups: What is your ambition in life? Do you, for instance, want to be a reporter? Or do you want to be editorial-page editor of the *Wall Street Journal*? I was sure I didn't want to be a reporter, especially not at the *Wall Street Journal*, where most reporters covered a single industry (insurance, airlines) or even a single company (AOL, Microsoft), had very few opportunities to comfort the afflicted, and never detached themselves from their cell phones. And even though a part of me did want to be editorial-page editor of the *Wall Street Journal*, which was the same thing as saying I wanted to be the Most Important Person at the World's Most Important Publication, I knew I never would be, because I didn't believe any of the things Bob Bartley believed. If I said no, he might be insulted. If I said yes, a part of him would always suspect that repairing split infinitives was merely the first step in my devious plan to succeed him, after which I would install a cadre of liberal editorial writers who would call for higher taxes on rich people, the abolition of nuclear weapons, and government-sponsored extramarital fellatio for all American Democrats.

I chose my words carefully. I said, No, I want to write a novel.

My answer pleased him, as I figured it would. When I left Bob Bartley's office, I knew I had the job.

Shortly thereafter, I ceased to hand out faxes, and instead wrote headlines and edited copy for the next three years. I was anonymous, efficient, and discreet. Nothing slipped past me. Day after day an unblemished page was shipped electronically to seventeen printing plants across the country, and the following morning nearly two million readers held the fruits of my labor in their hands. At first I resented the lack of attention paid my mastery of English grammar and the intricacies of the house style book. Not once did I receive a letter from an armchair grammarian in Dubuque or Terre Haute, one of those retired English teachers who scour the daily paper with a red pen in hand, searching for evidence of American decline in the form of a split infinitive. Nor did my immediate superior mention, even in passing, that I did my job diligently and well. But over time I began to take delight in this peculiar feature of my job – that my success was measured by how rarely people noticed what I did. In this way I believed myself akin to oil-tanker captains and air-traffic controllers, those anonymous technicians of social stability whose identities become known only through catastrophic failure.

When I moved to the Leisure & Arts page, I assumed I'd have little contact with the editorial writers. I was wrong. My cubicle was situated smack in the midst of theirs. A couple of them came forward to welcome me, but most of them didn't. The ones who welcomed me overlooked the fact that my politics were repugnant. Those who didn't welcome me couldn't overlook that fact. By hanging a campaign poster of Ralph Nader in my cubicle, I made it a hard fact to overlook.

I had almost nothing in the way of social interaction with the editorial writers, although I began to read their writing very closely, sometimes even dipping into the archives to sample their obsessions over the decades. They wrote with the zeal of converts, as if they'd all been Communists in their youth, and each of them clutched, with merciless loins, the flanks of a favorite right-wing hobby horse: not only taxes and weapons but the treachery and moral lassitude of the Palestinians, the creeping fascism of fluoride in the water supply, the heroic necessity of Pinochet's bloody dictatorship in crushing democratic socialism in Chile. In this way the collective voice of the newspaper, the unsigned editorials, was always the furthest to the right of the range of beliefs held by the editorial-page writers, no accident on Bob Bartley's part. He himself held the most extreme position on every issue, and although he couldn't write three editorials a day himself, he took great care in his choice of surrogates. He hired people who could just as well have been Republican speechwriters, as indeed some of them had been (Peggy Noonan) or soon would be (Bill McGurn) – a line of work that seemed to me, if not exactly noble, then at least more intellectually honest than masquerading as a journalist.

I tried once and only once to engage in a reasonable discussion about politics with one of the editorial writers. She was a voluble and attractive young blonde who'd grown up in Oregon and gone to college at Princeton. She worked in the cubicle next to mine. She wrote a lot about environmental issues, and one time I told her I disagreed with something she'd written about federal forest policy. The essence of my argument was simple: I don't think trees should be cut down carelessly. She told me that trees existed to be cut down. Needless to say, I was surprised; I sort of assumed people from Oregon liked trees. She said she preferred clear-cuts – essentially, forests transformed into nonforests. She said that clear-cuts grew back as peaceful meadows, which were aesthetically superior to forests. I disagreed. She said I had an unhealthy, sentimental attitude about trees; she accused me of wanting to hug them. I told her I didn't want to hug them, I just didn't think they should all die. But she said most trees would be better off dead, after which they could be given a more useful second life as chairs, ranch houses, or fax paper.

We didn't talk much after that, although we always said hello when passing in the hallways.

My boss, Raymond Sokolov, was the one true sophisticate among the bunch. He'd founded, in 1982, the Leisure & Arts page as a daily staple of the paper. Before that he'd been a book and movie critic for *Newsweek*, a food editor at the *New York Times*, and a columnist for *Natural History* magazine. He'd also written several books, among them a biography of A. J. Liebling. With his diminutive stature, his shock of white hair, and his colorful bow ties, he had the appearance of a mischievous, elfin intellectual. He was no ideologue when it came to politics. He seemed, from what I could gather in our occasional, brief conversations, to be a sensible moderate, but he had a streak of iconoclasm, some inherent desire to tweak the sensibilities of the powers that be.

One day he came to me with a proposal. Our regular TV critic was going on vacation. Would I care to try my hand at filling her column? I could pick through the piles of tapes she was sent by the networks and write on anything that struck me, as long as he approved it first.

I was flattered – but I hadn't owned a television in seven years. This, I told him, might rob me of the requisite tone of authority, the breadth of reference, that is the currency of the modern newspaper critic.

He stroked the tips of his mustache with his thumb and forefinger and sagely nodded his head. Why don't you write about life without television? he said. For one day we can make the TV column an anti-TV column. He flashed a devilish smile. The next week, for the first time in anyone's memory, the paper's TV column failed to offer a blurb for the latest darling project of some cable or network exec. Nor did it provide *Fortune* 500 ad managers with a hint of where to place their commercials. Nothing was hyped or sold. In fact, a half-dozen subscribers wrote letters to the editor and claimed they'd been emboldened to unplug their sets and stow them away in their attics. And while all of this gave me a small but palpable thrill, it may have been that assignment that first helped me move beyond a conception of myself as a hardworking and dedicated foe of split infinitives and run-on sentences, an honest working stiff in the salt mines of American journalism. My little column suddenly helped me see myself through the eyes of the men in the suites upstairs: another peon doing his part to enhance shareholder value at the flagship editorial product in the universe of Dow Jones brands. So this peon doesn't have a TV set. How droll.

Nonetheless, the paper had an audience of millions, and a part of me couldn't quite shake the idea that the point of writing is to have your work read by as many people as possible. So, once a month or so, I'd propose an article for the Leisure & Arts page, and more often than not Ray would go for it. In this manner I smuggled the occasional outré sentiment into the paper.

The assignment I enjoyed most was a profile of a radical black performance artist named William Pope.L. He'd once walked the streets of Harlem with a twelve-foot white phallus strapped to his midsection, a comment on white fears of black sexuality that sent the National Endowment for the Arts – which had once bestowed on Pope.L a grant of taxpayer money – into a tizzy. His most famous work, however, involved eating a copy of the *Wall Street Journal* with the aid of ketchup and milk, then regurgitating the meal, all while sitting on a gleaming porcelain toilet perched atop a ten-foot scaffold. He told me he'd once seen an ad campaign for the paper that made it out to be the modern equivalent of a primitive cultural object imbued with mystical powers. I quoted his explanation at length: 'The ads suggested that if you bought a subscription, good things would happen to you. It proposed that the paper could have magical effects. You didn't have to read it. Just having it near you, having it land on your doorstep, would multiply your wealth.

So I took the logic to its absurd conclusion. Shouldn't ingesting it increase your wealth ten-fold?'

It was Ray's idea to run the piece on the day the paper, after more than a hundred years in existence, first enlivened its pages with color ink. Thus I could quip that we'd spiced up the product mainly for the sake of its digestibility. Nothing I wrote elicited more comments from my colleagues, and everyone thought it was a gas.

Bob Bartley and I talked so infrequently I remember every occasion with total clarity. I even recorded these encounters in my journal, for posterity and biographers. The first time, he asked if I would proofread something he'd written. I didn't want to proofread his editorials. I thought they were wrong; copyediting would only prettify their idiocy. But you don't say no to the Most Important Person at the World's Most Important Publication. The people who usually proofread his editorials were gone for the day, and apparently I was the only one left in the office who knew how to repair dangling participles.

I read the editorial. I disagreed with everything in it, but it was powerfully written. That's the thing about his editorials – even if you thought they were wrong, they left you with no doubt about what he believed. He claimed to craft everything he wrote for optimal 'muzzle velocity,' as he once put it to another journalist. His style owed a great deal to the old yellow journalism of personal invective, and he didn't just savage his opponents' ideas, he aimed to obliterate his opponents altogether.

I told him I saw only one mistake. It wasn't a split infinitive, it was an unsplit word. He'd made the words 'pipe dream' one word, with no space between them. I told him it should be two words, according to Webster's *New World Dictionary*, which was my authoritative source in such matters.

He told me he didn't care what Webster's *New World Dictionary* said. It was his editorial, and he wanted 'pipe dream' to be one word. He said I should delete the space I'd inserted between 'pipe' and 'dream.'

I did.

I never edited anything by Bob Bartley again.

We talked a second time a few months later. I was standing in the hallway with some colleagues from the Leisure & Arts page, and Bob Bartley approached us. He said he had two doctors' appointments on the Upper East Side of Manhattan the next day. He had a bit of leisure time to spare between them and wondered if there was any art at the museums on the Upper East Side that he ought to see.

I said, Yes, there's a wonderful show of Walker Evans photos at the Met. Anyone who cares about photography – or America – should see it if he can.

He said, Thanks, I may just go.

A few days later I met him in the hallway. I said hello. He did not say hello.

I said, Bob, did you see the Walker Evans show at the Met? He stopped and looked at me. I wondered if I should have called him Mr. Bartley instead of Bob.

He said, Yes, I saw it.

What did you think? I asked.

It wasn't for me, he said. I stayed for five minutes and went to the Egyptian galleries.

After I thought about it for a while, his answer made sense. Walker Evans was the great documentarian of Depression-era Southern poverty; Bob Bartley was appalled by the very idea of poor people. In fact, he'd once said he didn't think there were any poor people left in America – 'just a few hermits or something like that.' (This quote can be found in the *Washington Post Magazine* of July 11, 1982.) On this issue Bob Bartley was the intellectual heir of an old American idea expressed most succinctly by the preacher Henry Ward Beecher: 'No man in this land suffers from poverty unless it be more than his fault – unless it be his *sin*.' For Bob Bartley, the agrarian pictures of Walker Evans and the homoerotic pictures of Robert Mapplethorpe were morally equivalent. Both depicted human beings in a sinful state of filth and degradation, and such images had no place in an American museum.

Of course I disagreed. Not only did I appreciate the unadorned honesty of Walker Evans's photographs, I'd grown up in a poor family myself. As a child, while living on a rented farm where we struggled to make enough money to feed ourselves, I'd stood in line with my mother for handouts of surplus government cheese. Pictures of people like us from the time of the Great Depression hung in many museums, a testament to certain unappealing aspects of the American experience.

Bob Bartley didn't believe the government should be in the cheese-handout business.

I never recommended a museum to Bob Bartley again.

The last time we spoke was on the day of his retirement. Dow Jones & Company required senior executives to retire at the age of 65. Bob Bartley was now 65, and would be replaced as editorial-page editor by Paul Gigot, who'd won a Pulitzer Prize for commentary and often appeared on the *News Hour with Jim Lehrer* on PBS. Paul Gigot wrote signed columns that made him sound like a reasonable conservative, although some of his unsigned pieces hinted at a fear that the Boy Scouts might soon become a front group for initiating American boys in the fine art of fellatio. As for Bob Bartley, he would still write a weekly column called 'Thinking Things Over,' in which he would say the same things he'd been thinking for thirty years all over again.

I went to the men's room on my way out of the office. Bob Bartley was in the men's room too. We stood next to each other, pissing contemplatively, not talking. When I was finished, I went to the sink and washed my hands. When Bob Bartley was finished, he looked at himself in the mirror and walked out.

We boarded the elevator together. His hair was mussed, and his shoulders were slumped. He had the doleful look of an injured horse aware it's about to be taken out to pasture and shot.

Big day, I said.

Yes, he said.

I thought a little flattery might cheer him up.

Now Paul gets to see how hard you work, I said.

That's right, he said. And I have to figure out how to disengage. Not sure how to do that. Maybe stop coming into the office every day.

Yes, I said, I can imagine that would be a challenge after thirty years.

He didn't respond.

As we got off the elevator, I tried to think of something else to say to him – something serious and substantive, something intelligent people may have wanted to ask him but were too afraid – since I knew I'd probably never speak to him again. I considered asking him how he felt about an in-depth study of his editorials by the *Columbia Journalism Review*, which found that his page 'rarely offers balance, is often unfair, and is riddled with errors – distortions and outright falsehoods of every kind and stripe.' I thought to ask whether he felt in any way responsible for the death of Vincent Foster, the White House counsel to Bill Clinton who'd killed himself shortly after Bob Bartley ran a series of harsh attacks on his integrity. A note found in Foster's briefcase expressed anguish that 'the *WSJ* editors lie without consequence.' After Foster's death, Bob Bartley's editorials hinted darkly that Foster may have been murdered for knowing too much about Whitewater, and called for a special counsel to investigate. 'The American public is entitled to know if Mr. Foster's death was somehow connected to his high office,' Bob Bartley wrote. I sort of thought the American public was entitled to know if Bob Bartley thought Vince Foster's death was somehow connected to irresponsible journalism.

In my heart I knew it was the wrong day for such questions, so I didn't ask them. We parted ways in the lobby, him heading for his limousine to Brooklyn, me for the subway to Queens.

Well, I said, enjoy your newfound freedom.

I'll try, he said.

I never talked to Bob Bartley again.

Ray's most provocative move had nothing to do with my writing for the paper. It was March of 2000 when he hatched a plan to get a poet friend of his the exposure Ray thought he deserved. The poet's name was Frederick Seidel. I'd never heard of him. Ray said he was brilliant but had a devil of a time getting started on a poem; in fact, in a review in the late '80s, Ray had called him 'gifted' but 'maddeningly unproductive.' Ray's plan was to give Seidel a monthly deadline, as if he were a journalist. Seidel would write one poem a month under the title of that month, and not only would the deadline prod him into action, the paper would offer him an audience the size of which most poets could only dream.

Here, Ray said, reaching into his bookshelves. Take these home with you. See what you think.

I spent that evening with three of Seidel's collections. Some of it was profoundly beautiful, like this, from a poem called 'The Childhood Sunlight' in his book *The Cosmos Poems*:

> The parking lot washed clean smells sweet,
> And even has a rainbow that
> A little girl tiptoes toward,
> Hoping not to frighten it.
>
> The neighbor's dog that won't go home
> Is watching her – which she can't see –
> With naked eyes of love and awe.
> She feels that way herself sometimes.
>
> When you are sure that you're alone,
> Tell yourself to not be sure.
> This universe is not the first.
> The other ones are not the same.

This sort of poem was atypical, though. Generally, reading Seidel was like riding shotgun on a Ducati racer, a machine that appeared on occasion in his poems. It was a ride full of quick, propulsive accelerations and sudden, screeching stops, hairpin turns into spooky alleys. In addition to racing bikes there was a lot of racy sex. Ray could not have picked a poet better suited to offend the sensibilities of wealthy born-again housewives or buttoned-up corporate executives in the great American suburbs.

Seidel began to write his poems, one per month, and it was my job to typeset them, make sure all the italics and em-dashes and capital letters were just so, and then fax him a copy to inspect and approve. When we talked on the phone, I felt like a peasant in the presence of royalty. He always said, Phil, my boy, how are you? in the most sophisticated voice I'd ever heard, very precise, as if his concourse was always with the gods but he'd learned English as a second language, so he could order lunch. He always wanted to know what I thought of his poems. What could I tell him? I was on deadline every time, late in the afternoon, with headlines to write and stories to cut to make them fit on the page. I didn't have time to read his poems the half-dozen times required for me to make sense of them, at least not until the next morning, before the hum of the day began, when I could sit with a cup of coffee and my feet up on my desk, reading the paper. What I really wanted to say was, Dude, I can't believe you're getting away with this in the *Wall Street Journal*! You're my hero! But that seemed a little lowbrow, so I'd focus on a particular stanza whose music I liked, or a particular image that struck me. I think he believed I wasn't a very bright boy, at least when it came to poetry.

My favorite of his early poems for the paper was this:

DECEMBER

My Christmas is covered
With goosepimples in the cold.
Her arms are raised straight
Above her head.

She turns around slowly in nothing but a
Garter belt and stockings outdoors.
She has the powerful
Buttocks of a Percheron.

My beautiful with goosepimples
Climbs the ladder to the high diving board
In her high heels
And ideals.

The mirror of the swimming pool is looking up at her
Round breasts.
She bounces up and down
As if about to dive.

In her ideals, in her high heels,
The palm trees go up and down.
The mirror of the swimming pool is looking up at her
Bikini trim.

The heated swimming pool mirror is steaming
In the cold.
The Christmas tree is on.
A cigarette speedboat cuts the bay in two.

It rears up on its white wake.
Ay, Miami!
Ninety miles away
Is Mars.

The cigarette smokes fine cigars,
Rolls hundred dollar bills into straws.
My Christmas
Is in his arms.

Around this time, not surprisingly, there began to be heard complaints about the political thrust and aesthetic sensibilities of the Leisure & Arts page. Ray mentioned these complaints to me in elliptical asides to conversations on other matters. He'd apparently been forwarded some scolding letters to the editor about a couple of Seidel poems; he'd also received a memo from the publisher that raised concerns about propriety and sound judgment. But Ray was a cagey fellow, a survivor of twenty years in the shadow of Bob Bartley, and although I never asked him how he responded to questions about his stewardship, I imagined him pointing out that the occasional kerfuffle proved he had his readers' attention, and besides, every single day a big fat ad appeared on his page. For a time he managed to forestall these complaints, in part because the paper was awash in ad money.

We were, after all, in the midst of millennial madness. The paper was both an avid chronicler of and an unashamed participant in that madness, and, as Bob Bartley believed and Ray was aware, a balance sheet deep in the black was the strongest proof of virtue known to man.

One month after I was originally hired, the Dow Jones Industrial Average – comprising thirty companies chosen by the managing editor of the *Wall Street Journal*, and the only company brand more recognizable than the paper itself – closed above 10,000 for the first time. The paper celebrated this triumph with a banner six-column headline, only the third in its history, the others having blared the news of the bombing of Pearl Harbor and the start of the first Gulf War.

Nearly a year to the day after I began at the paper, the NASDAQ index reached an all-time high of 5048.62. The paper was so fat with 'New Economy' advertising, the average subscriber – white, fiftyish, male, with a yearly household income of around $200,000 – risked a hernia when he lifted it off his doorstep. Management went on a hiring spree to fill an ever greater need for copy to offset the profusion of ads. The paper started whole new daily sections and weekly supplements to cash in on the marketing lucre of companies that would go belly up before the end of their second fiscal year. I knew colleagues who charged every movie, every dinner, every new book and bottle of high-end wine to company credit cards. Ad managers at the paper's sister publication, *Barron's*, were known to keep open tabs at various Manhattan bars and to entertain clients by expensing the cost of strippers. No one in the suites batted an eye. Company executives merely increased their own bonuses.

It was easy to be carried along on this tide of giddy prosperity, writing the occasional mildly subversive piece in order to cling, however tenuously, to what I thought of as possession of my soul. I made a salary in the mid-five figures, more than I'd ever expected. I saw jazz for free in any club I cared to visit, just by calling ahead and telling the doorman where I worked. When I wrote a profile of a writer or a musician – Larry McMurtry, Jacky Terrasson – the subject's latest book or album shot up the Amazon.com sales charts. I was moving units and meeting people.

I built a sweet little home library from the spoils of the weekly book give-away, the constant pile of review copies sent by American publishers to the paper's book editor. Not only did I make off with reissued classics from Penguin and the Modern Library, I surreptitiously swiped the volumes on Tantric sex, slipping them into my bag when no one else was looking. When uttered during the exchange of small talk at parties in Brooklyn tenements – always somewhat sheepishly, and only in response to direct questions about my gainful employment – the words *Wall Street Journal* had the effect of a good narcotic: dilated pupils, flushed face, and what seemed to me a perceptible slackening of sexual inhibition, which, being a shy and socially awkward young man from the American Middle West, I never did take advantage of, despite my collection of books on Tantric sex.

You might think an institution whose very purpose is to chronicle the ups and downs of American capitalism would be uniquely prepared for a swing in the business cycle. You would be wrong. Dow Jones was notoriously bad at running its own business. In the late 1980s, the company bought an electronic provider of business information called Telerate for $1.6 billion. It was meant to compete with Reuters and Bloomberg. A decade later, Dow Jones sold Telerate at a loss of almost $1 billion. The 'New Economy' boom was a chimera that allowed the company to believe it might escape the shackles of Telerate and its other dumb decisions, but the sudden implosion of tech stocks in 2000 hit Dow Jones like a blow to the solar plexus. Ad revenue plummeted. Managers at the flagship editorial product in the universe of Dow Jones brands were instructed to streamline their budgets. In the summer of 2001 we received a memo that said the following:

Dear Ladies and Gentlemen, We are discontinuing the ownership and maintenance of indoor plants throughout our office space in the World Financial Center. This, combined with a similar move in South Brunswick, will save Dow Jones more than $40,000 per year. The WFC plants will be moved from the floor space to the reception areas for disposal late Friday, July 13, 2001. If you would like to take over the maintenance of any of the plants, please attach a yellow Post-It note with your name to a visible part of the plant container. Or, if you would like to take any of the plants home, please feel free to do so before this Friday, July 13. If you have any questions, please call Bill at ext. 2072.

This was a novel form of outsourcing, I thought.

At the time, Dow Jones CEO Peter Kann made almost $2 million per year in salary and bonuses. In his glory days, he and his wife had been known to fly to the office in a helicopter from their home in New Jersey. I wondered whether the company could just get rid of Peter Kann – it had already jettisoned the helicopter – and save the indoor plants. But I never said anything.

Other ominous things happened. We received a memo from Peter Kann in which he wrote: 'As most of you know, over the last two or three weeks we have done a number of layoffs in some parts of the company as part of a cost-reduction program aimed at getting our expense structure aligned with reduced revenues in a tougher business environment.'

Peter Kann had once been a journalist. In the 1970s, he'd won a Pulitzer Prize as a foreign correspondent for the *Wall Street Journal.* Moving to the suites had hampered his prose style, but if you read the memo enough times, you could figure out what he was saying. He was saying: Since I'm not giving back my $1 million New Economy bonus, lots of people are getting canned.

He later named his wife to replace him as publisher of the *Wall Street Journal*, a rather brazen bit of nepotism, I thought, but I never said anything.

Things got worse. There were rumors the company would be sold to a competitor – the *New York Times*, the *Washington Post*. In the office cafeteria, reporters and editors had the look of a dwindling tribe being hunted by enemies with superior weaponry.

The atmosphere around the office was clammy with portents of doom.

On September 11, 2001, just as I finished my breakfast, I received a call from a friend who knew I lived without a TV. She told me, in a voice wracked with panic, that the World Trade Center towers had been hit by airplanes. I put on my suit jacket, left my apartment, and ran to take a subway to work. I was on journalistic autopilot: there was a big story, I was within reach of the story – it was right across the street from my workplace – and therefore I had a professional obligation to get there, even if I usually copyedited pieces about theater and books.

Partway to the office, my train stalled and didn't

move for an hour and a half. Since we were stuck underground, we had no way of knowing the severity of the situation downtown, and when at last we were discharged from the train at Union Square, I continued the journey to the office on foot. In Chinatown, the police had cordoned off the streets. No one was allowed any farther, not even people with press credentials, although as a copy editor I had none. The towers, in the distance, were swathed in a cloud of black smoke; my mind, still stuck in a news vacuum, couldn't comprehend that they no longer stood, though in fact they'd fallen an hour earlier. I did know that if I was truly intent on getting to the office, I had but one choice. I would have to reenter the subway system and walk through the tunnel.

The entrance to the Franklin Street station was blocked with yellow police tape. I looked at the campaign posters for the mayoral primary taped to the railing above the stairs and thought that, if I crossed the police line, there would be no one to rely on thereafter but myself. What else was I going to do? Go back to my apartment and listen to the radio? Sit in a bar and watch TV? I lifted the tape, descended the stairs, and, in a last gesture toward civilized norms, swiped my MetroCard instead of jumping the turnstile.

No trains were running. No clerk was in the token booth. I waited a few moments to see if a train or an MTA worker would appear, but there was only an otherworldly quiet. With no one around to stop me,

I lowered myself onto the tracks and began walking through the tunnel, creeping through the dark, careful to avoid touching the third rail. Not even the squeak of a rat marred the silence. It would be the only time I ever heard nothing in New York.

Ten blocks later, when I emerged into the light of the Chambers Street station, the platform was coated in dust, and ahead in the tunnel I heard water rushing with a sound like a waterfall. A couple of cops were in the station, hanging around the token booth. I waited until they wandered off and then I climbed the stairs to the street.

I emerged a couple of blocks north of the towers, or at least where the towers had been. The streets were covered in ash and office paper. A cop stood alone in the middle of the street, watching a burning building, which I later learned was World Trade Center number seven. I walked over and stood next to her, both of us mesmerized. After a couple of minutes she looked at me. That building's probably gonna go, she said, you might wanna get outta here. She didn't order me to leave. She seemed to assume I wouldn't. She merely offered it as a suggestion, one among a series of options, take it or leave it.

I picked up a discarded dust mask, put it on my face, and began to make my way around the smoking rubble, through streets flooded with greenish-yellow water, or ankle-deep in fine gray powder. After crossing the West Side Highway, I entered the World Financial

Center complex. The Winter Garden's glass roof was shattered in places, and the palm trees in the court-yard were pallid with ash. All the shops were empty. I climbed the emergency fire stairs in World Financial Center building number one. No one was there. The office had long been evacuated and was now, at least on our floors, coated in a thin gritty film blown in through shattered windows, though the computers still ran on the power of a backup generator. It was one of the most unnerving moments of my life, standing in that empty newsroom, wondering where everyone was, hoping none of my colleagues had been hurt or killed, all those computers humming with no one in front of them.

I went to my cubicle, blew the ash off my key-board, set a newspaper over the dust on my chair, and logged on to my computer. I sent an e-mail mes-sage to the entire editorial-page staff, asking if anyone needed anything, since I'd made it to the office. Those equipped with laptops immediately wrote back and told me I was crazy, that I ought to get the hell out as soon as possible, there was nothing I could do for them there, a gas line might explode, the building might collapse. I logged off and walked around the office, inspecting the damage, hoping I might see another editor or reporter, but I couldn't find a soul. I circled back to my desk. The telephone rang. It sounded a lit-tle forlorn, even spooky, amid the unusual silence of the newsroom. I picked it up. It was my mother calling from Texas, where she was on vacation with my father, watching TV with her in-laws. I could tell from her voice that she was frightened witless. I said I was fine, we were just now evacuating the building, all was well, I would call her later in the afternoon. I hung up and checked my voice mail. There were eight frantic messages from friends wondering if I was OK. I got up and went to the men's room. I felt strangely reverent as I stood before the urinal, aware I'd be the last man to piss there that day, that week, perhaps even that month or longer. (Almost a year, as it turned out.) The irony, when I thought about it later, was vertiginous: I had less devotion to the idea of the paper than anyone else I knew there, yet I'd risked my safety to get to the office – and for nothing. I was useless. Little did I know that if I'd wanted to be of help I should have hopped a ferry to New Jersey, where a small group of editors was putting together a paper that would win a Pulitzer Prize for spot news coverage. The *Wall Street Journal* of September 12, 2001 carried the fourth banner headline in the paper's history, in letters nearly as big as the masthead: 'TERRORISTS DESTROY WORLD TRADE CENTER, HIT PENTAGON IN RAID WITH HIJACKED JETS.'

I suppose I could tell you how the smoke smelled when I went back outside, like every kind of burning you've ever known in your life rolled into a cloud so thick you could almost drink it. I suppose I could tell you how, if you looked up at the bright blue sky a certain way, you could see waves of tiny glass crystals floating and sparkling like iridescent sea anemones. I could also tell you about the firefighters standing around in the smoke and dust, holding their heads in their hands, some of them openly weeping. But I've already gone on too long. Hundreds of people have written about what they saw on September 11, and I have nothing to add to that. I was just another of the spectators at the edge of the rubble, vainly hoping for a call to join a rescue operation, snapping pictures with a digital camera I'd snatched from the office, as if to preserve in some other form, outside of myself, the ghastly images searing themselves on my brain.

For a few weeks we all commuted to the cornfields of New Jersey. We put out the paper in a makeshift newsroom, a windowless bunker in the training wing of Dow Jones corporate headquarters near Princeton. My commute was two hours each way. All the stories in the paper concerned terrorism. It felt, for a time, utterly asinine to have anything to do with leisure and art. After anthrax turned up in the offices of other media companies, all of our mail was heat-steamed. The men in the mail room sorted it with masks on their faces and rubber gloves on their hands. They looked like lab technicians working with a deadly poison. When we opened our mail, the envelopes crackled like dead leaves, and the ink on the letters was often illegible.

When Danny Pearl was abducted in Pakistan, most of us had an inkling how that would end, and we braced ourselves. On the day we learned he'd been beheaded, you could have heard a pin drop in the office. He was entirely the wrong man for such a fate – not to say that there's a right man. But he wasn't a slavering ideologue. He wasn't a rhetorical flamethrower who never left the home office. He was out in the danger zones, seeking to understand radical Islam by talking to the people who were shaping and being shaped by it. He believed in the democratic function of storytelling. The horror of his end was unimaginable.

About the only thing in the paper that made much sense anymore was Fred Seidel's monthly poem. All the news stories tracking terrorist recruiting and finances, all the editorials calling for 'total war' and a full-scale invasion of the Middle East in response to September 11 – all of it seemed inadequate next to those eight monthly stanzas of Seidel's verse, which, by adopting a voice as twisted and chilling as that of Osama bin Laden, seemed to get much closer to the heart of the matter. Consider this, written two months after the attacks:

I don't believe in anything, I do
Believe in you.
Down here in hell we do don't.
I can't think of anything I won't.

I amputate your feet and I walk.
I excise your tongue and I talk.
You make me fly through the black sky.
I will kill you until I die.

Thank God for you, God.
I do.
My God, it is almost always Christmas Eve this time of
year, too.
Then I began to pray.

I don't believe in anything anyway.
I did what I do. I do believe in you.
Down here in hell they do don't.
I can't think of anything we won't.

How beautiful thy feet with shoes.
Struggling barefoot over dunes of snow forever, more
falling, forever, Jews
Imagine mounds of breasts stretching to the horizon.
We send them to their breast, mouthful of orison.

I like the color of the smell. I like the odor of spoiled meat.
I like how gangrene transubstantiates warm firm flesh
into rotten sleet.
When the blue blackens and they amputate, I fly.
I am flying a Concorde of modern passengers to
gangrene in the sky.

I am flying to Area Code 212
To stab a Concorde into you,
To plunge a sword into the gangrene.
This is a poem about a sword of kerosene.

This is my 21st century in hell.
I stab the sword into the smell.
I am the sword of sunrise flying into Area Code 212
To flense the people in the buildings, and the buildings,
into dew.

Needless to say, some of the paper's more sensitive readers were not impressed; they wrote letters calling for Seidel to be silenced.

Now when I wrote for the paper the stakes were higher, and with Fred as my, dare I say, moral example – the writer willing to say the unsayable in a climate of fear and self-censorship – I chose my subjects with the utmost care. Still, it was easier as a journalist: I could simply quote the words of others, neither condoning nor condemning. In a profile of jazz trumpeter Dave Douglas, for instance, I quoted him calling the war in Afghanistan 'more of a trade show and a laboratory for new weapons than a real pursuit of those who perpetrated that horrible event' already known by the glib shorthand 9/11. But it wasn't as if the paper's readers were looking to the arts pages for an understanding of what would soon be christened 'the war on terror.'

Once we were resettled in Manhattan, in temporary quarters above the West Side's Garment District, the men in the suites looked again for places to squeeze. Eventually a quarter of the company's workforce would be cut, and Ray was among the downsized. At the age of 60, after twenty years of service to the company, he was strong-armed to take early retirement and replaced by a guy who'd cut his journalistic teeth at the Moonie-owned *Washington Times*.

Soon it came to pass that I was given a chance to

work on pieces of greater world-political import. I was sitting with my feet on my desk, editing a story about a play in Chicago, or an opera in Seattle, or maybe the lovely wines of the Alsace region, when Paul Gigot asked me to follow him into an empty conference room. He invited me to sit. He cut straight to the chase. He said that for the foreseeable future I would continue copyediting for the Leisure & Arts page, but beginning in a few weeks I would do the same for the editorial page of the *Wall Street Journal*'s European edition.

I told him I didn't want to do that.

He seemed surprised.

I told him I didn't agree with the politics of the editorial page.

He said he wasn't asking me to write things I didn't believe. He was asking me to delete serial commas and repair split infinitives.

I told him I didn't want my hands on the editorial page in any way, shape, or form.

He said he would give me a small raise in compensation for my added responsibilities, and I would do whatever he told me to do.

I thanked him for the raise.

I'd been keeping another folder, much like the one I'd called 'GREATEST HITS OF PUBLIC RELATIONS,' though the title on this one said 'FULL-BLOWN INSANITY ON THE *WSJ* EDITORIAL PAGE,' and when

I got home that night I opened it and read the clippings again, slowly. I'd known all along there would come a time when I'd need them, and this was it.

On the day after September 11, an editorial stated: 'We are entitled to presume that this is the work of the usual suspects – Saddam Husein,' et cetera. Two days later a news article in the paper reported that 'U.S. Officials Discount Any Role by Iraq in Terrorist Attacks.' The editorial page was unruffled. 'Reports are swirling,' an unsigned piece announced the next day, 'that Saddam Hussein was also behind last week's attacks . . . Deposing Saddam has to be considered another war aim.'

Immediately the paper called for speeding up the deployment of a missile-defense shield – an effort that seemed to me like that of a man lifting an umbrella over his head while being pelted in the groin by snowballs. An unsigned editorial argued that the first and most important steps in combatting terrorism ought to include capital-gains tax cuts and immediate drilling for oil in the Arctic National Wildlife Refuge. The same editorial stated: 'Throughout history the periods of greatest military innovation have been wars.' Apparently war was needed, because military innovation was needed, because nineteen men had flown passenger jets into three buildings on American soil. I didn't follow the logic but I could see where this was headed. On and on it went. October 4: 'Clinton Didn't Do Enough to Stop Terrorists,' under the byline of painmed addict Rush Limbaugh. October 9: 'The Answer to Terrorism? Colonialism.'

It was clear they wouldn't stop clamoring until they got themselves an honest-to-God war.

After I'd read all the clippings and put them aside, I was acutely aware that if I removed so much as one serial comma from an editorial calling for 'total war,' capital-gains tax cuts, or the despoiling of wildlife refuges in response to September 11, I would find myself chin-deep in a malodorous swamp of hypocrisy. Here, finally, was the line I could not cross. After promptly using my allotment of yearly paid vacation, I served notice that I was terminating my employment at the World's Most Important Publication, ostensibly to finish work on a novel which did not, in fact, exist. Instead I arranged to take a seasonal job in New Mexico as a fire lookout with the United States Forest Service, an appropriate form of penance, really, that involved alerting authorities when trees caught on fire, so crews could come and save them. Alone in my little bird's nest, my glass-walled perch, I would add almost nothing to the gross national product, which was gross enough on its own.

I met Paul Gigot in the hallway on my second-to-last day of work, and we had one last brief conversation, which I recorded in my journal for posterity and biographers.

Well, it's been a pleasure, I said.

Yes, good luck, he said.

At least now you'll be able to hire someone who's more enthusiastic about working on the editorial page, I said.

Oh, we decided against that plan, he said.

Whoever replaces you is only going to work on Leisure & Arts.

He stepped onto the elevator and threw me a little half-wave, half-salute.

So long, he said.

As a connoisseur of subterfuge and stealth – having earned my original position at the paper by means of manipulating the truth to my advantage – I at first had the thought that I'd been purged by my own hand, by a pure ballsy bluff. This would have been in keeping with the whole mind-set of the editorial page – that their enemies were treasonous, despicable, and deserving of nothing but ruination and contempt. But I didn't want to think like them. I didn't want to share in their paranoia. I wanted, in the end, to believe it had been miscommunication, a mistake. (Oh, it had been a mistake all right, from the very beginning.) And anyway, what was I going to do? Take it back? Beg him to let me stay?

So long, I said, waving.

[2006]

nh Notting Hill Editions

Notting Hill Editions is devoted to the best in essay writing. Our authors, living and dead, cover a broad range of non-fiction, but all display the virtues of brevity, soul and wit.

To discover more, please visit
www.nottinghilleditions.com

– Contributors –

Carla Blumenkranz is a co-editor of *n+1*.

Philip Connors is the author of *Fire Season: Field Notes from a Wilderness Lookout*. He lives in southwest New Mexico.

Kristin Dombek is a writer living in New York.

Christopher Glazek is a senior editor at *n+1*.

Alice Gregory is a writer living in New York.

A. S. Hamrah is the *n+1* film critic.

Lawrence Jackson is a professor of English and American Studies at Emory University. His latest book is *My Father's Name: A Black Virginia Family After the Civl War* (2012).

Nikil Saval is a co-editor of *n+1*. His book *Cubed: The Secret History of the Workplace* is forthcoming from Doubleday in April 2014.

Emily Witt is the author of a forthcoming book about the sex lives of American women.

Molly Young is a writer living in New York.

nh